START YOUR OWN RELIGION

The Author

Colin Morris worked for many years as a Methodist missionary in Northern Rhodesia, now Zambia. He was a close friend and supporter of Kenneth Kaunda, and was elected the First President of the United Church of Zambia.

In 1970 he came back to Britain, and worked as Minister of Wesley's Chapel, London, was elected President of the British Methodist Conference, and became General Secretary of the Overseas Division of the Methodist Church. In 1978 he joined the BBC, first as Head of Religious Television, then, from 1980, as Head of Religious Broadcasting. He was Controller of BBC Northern Ireland between 1987 and 1991. He is now Director of the Centre for Religious Communication at Westminster College, Oxford.

He has written many books, among them *Include Me Out* (1968), *Unyoung, Uncoloured, Unpoor* (1969), *Wrestling with an Angel* (1971), *God in a Box* (1984), *Drawing the Line* (1987) and *Starting from Scratch* (1990).

Colin Morris

START YOUR OWN RELIGION

BBC BOOKS

This book is for
Pauline Webb
Always there, through thick and thin

Published by BBC Books,
a division of BBC Enterprises Limited,
Woodlands, 80 Wood Lane, London W12 0TT
First published 1992
© Colin Morris 1992

ISBN 0 563 36465 3

Set in 10/12pt Imprint by Redwood Press, Melksham
Printed and bound in Great Britain by Clays Ltd, St Ives Plc
Cover printed by Clays Ltd, St Ives Plc

CONTENTS

PREFACE

This book is an expanded version of ten talks I gave on BBC TV in the autumn of 1992. I was anxious to explore the nature of what might be called religion pure and simple, though I realise that in real life religion is never encountered in its pure form, and it is anything but simple. In order to get back to first principles, I came up with the DIY idea. If I were to start from scratch, taking for granted nothing in my upbringing and training and culture, how would I go about constructing my own religion – as an exercise in discovering what religion is and how it works. It seemed a straightforward enough thing to do – until I tried it.

But at least the discipline of trying to force religious ideas into the DIY mould caused me to wrestle with a number of issues to which I had given very little attention. I assumed that my Christian faith would take care of them as a matter of course. But probing beneath one's formal religious convictions is a little like stripping wallpaper, you are astounded at the patterns and texture of the layers that are revealed and the story they tell.

Reading through the manuscript, I note that when I mention religions other than Christianity I tend to concentrate on Judaism or Islam and steer well clear of Hinduism or Buddhism. That is not a value-judgement about 'higher' and 'lower' or 'primitive' and 'advanced' religions. I can make the imaginative leap from Christianity to the other religions which proclaim belief in one God. I just cannot imagine myself as a Hindu or a Buddhist – their conception of God is, for cultural reasons, very difficult for me. The religions of the Jordan are part of my heritage whereas those of the Ganges are not. That is my loss, and it explains why fairly early on in the exercise I choose the religions of one God as the model to be explored.

I need to make some acknowledgements. One friend, having read the manuscript, commented that all the authors I quote in the text are early twentieth century – there is no mention of a theologian writing now. That is almost true and I see no need to be embarrassed about the fact. It has always seemed to me odd that Christians whose foundation documents are almost two thousand years old should be thought old-fashioned if they refer to books written a few decades ago. The authors I drew on for ideas and occasionally quotations had one thing in common with me, though I'm not elevating myself to their league. They too had done some religious broadcasting. They had wrestled with the challenge of talking about religion over the air to the general public.

One of them, Professor John MacMurray, I stumbled on by accident. When I was the BBC's Head of Religious Broadcasting, out of sheer curiosity I got out whatever books are to be found in the BBC library relating to religious talks given on radio since the Corporation came into existence in the 1920s. C. S. Lewis's *Mere Christianity* and Herbert Butterfield's Reith lectures, *Christianity and History*, are famous examples. But I also came across a couple of books by a philosophy professor called MacMurray who as long ago as 1932 gave a series of broadcast talks called *Freedom in the Modern World*. I was so impressed that I tracked down his other books, one of which, *The Structure of Religious Experience*, was broadcast in 1936. I have drawn heavily on these works in a couple of chapters because I find his arguments self-evidently true. MacMurray's broadcasts date from the era of plus-fours, Oxford brogues and straw hats. So what? Simply, clearly and profoundly, he explores the nature of popular religion without using a single technical term. His primary authority was not the Bible nor the teaching of the Church but common sense. In their truth, clarity and simplicity, his ideas speak as much to our time as to the period when they were first broadcast.

Dorothy L. Sayers was another accomplished broadcaster. Apart from her persona as a detective story writer, she was chiefly known for her radio plays, *The Zeal of Thy House* and *The Man Born to be King*. But in 1941 she produced a closely reasoned essay, *The Mind of the Maker*, which used the creative process in writing as an analogy of the operation of the Divine mind in making the world. I found her account of the mechanics of that stupendous cosmic DIY operation most illuminating. I know of no more acute analysis of that strangely elusive quality, inspiration.

My third authority was the old war-horse himself, G. K. Chesterton, who for my money has been the outstanding apologist of popular Christianity in our century. Using a mind and pen of extraordinary suppleness, he could start from literally anywhere, the most mundane object imaginable – a bunch of keys or a matchbox – and with irresistible logic derive the whole of Christian doctrine from it. Give him two matchboxes and he would build a history of western civilisation as well. He could reduce the most complex religious idea to a single vivid image or a striking paradox. The careful scholar will qualify every statement with copious footnotes lest he be savaged to death for wild injudiciousness in the pages of the *Journal of Theological Studies*. The popular apologist has to take a chance – over-simplifying complex truth and affirming it in a clear confident voice. Then he takes what's coming to him. If his argument is shot to pieces under him, so be it. He picks himself up, dusts himself off and has another go. He has no personal pride at stake. The apostle Paul called it being a fool for Christ's sake. There has been no wiser fool than Chesterton this century.

Three of my colleagues at Westminster College, Oxford – the Principal, The Rev Dr Kenneth Wilson, Dr Bernard Farr and the Revd Dr Martin Groves – read the manuscript and in the nicest possible way put me right on a number of technical matters. Martha Caute, my editor at BBC Enterprises, combined charm, encouragement and efficiency in equal parts, and Helen Alexander, BBC TV's Editor of Religious Worship Programmes, and Ann Richardson, the Producer, having seen the possibilities in the basic theme, realised it on screen with their usual unflappability and professionalism. Finally, I try to acknowledge in the dedication of this book my debt to Dr Pauline Webb for forty years of personal friendship and close colleagueship. Otherwise, the responsibility for all that follows is mine alone.

Colin Morris

FOREWORD

On Being Incurably Religious

The statesman and orator Edmund Burke said, 'Man is constitutionally a religious animal.' Note that word 'constitutionally'. Burke used language with precision. He presumably meant that religion is not an optional extra in human nature like the ability to carry a tune or ride a bicycle. It is bred into our bone. Or as someone else has said, human beings are incurably religious. It is a big claim.

Consider: out of the primeval swamp a creature emerges who unlike the rest of the animal world seems not to be content with his physical surroundings. Alone of all creation, he reaches the limit of his senses and concludes, 'There is more than this; and this more is better.' Uniquely amongst living beings, he does not placidly accept things as they are. He parts company with his animal relations and begins a blundering search for Who Knows What? The Idea of God is born as an awareness of Something More, Something Other – a power, a force which though unseen holds some kind of sway over his fate. And this strange faculty has been passed down through countless generations to us.

No one has ever really explained why or how the physical universe could breed these other-worldly cravings in one of its creatures. The evolutionary road along which we have travelled doesn't seem to be able to explain religion; on the other hand, religion says it can explain the road along which we have travelled.

An aptitude for religion seems to be a universal characteristic of the human species. Not every individual has invariably been religious but religion has been found in all societies throughout history. Some scholars used to say this isn't so; that far from religion being universal, some tribes and peoples never showed any trace of it. But it is now generally agreed that such conclusions were the result of faulty observation by travellers and missionaries, or imperfect knowledge of strange languages and customs. Some cultures have been brilliantly successful at concealing their religion from visitors because strangers were thought unworthy to have access to sacred mysteries. Or maybe casual observers didn't even recognise unfamiliar forms of religion when they stumbled across them. The origins of religion may be a mystery but the fact that some form of it seems to have been universal suggests that humanity has perennially faced certain problems or had particular needs which could be met in no other way.

Amongst the creatures with this strange other-worldly hunger there have always been favoured individuals who seem to possess other-worldly knowledge. Call them evolutionary freaks or use the conventional word, saints; they have been prepared to make the demands of this other world the absolute basis of their lives, regardless of the cost. Saints are the most impressive practical proof that religion is of central importance in human life, that it works. And there is often a strange similarity about the moral values and life-styles of saints that transcends the wide variety of religious labels they wear.

It is a strange thing, then, that human beings have from the earliest times responded to a craving they don't understand and sought a being they cannot see, hear or touch and who in any normal understanding of language isn't there. Thus, if we heard someone was praying in the next room, went in and found he wasn't alone, we would take it for granted that whatever was there with him was *not* God because it had registered with our senses.

What else in the history of the human race has been as audacious as this: the willingness not just of individuals but of whole societies to commit everything including life itself to the search for the invisible? We humans are, in comparison with other inhabitants of the natural world, inconspicuous in size, slight in strength, transient in life-span and in many ways ill-equipped with the basic necessities of survival. From the beginning, we had to fight creatures stronger than ourselves, chase those that are swifter and outwit those more cunning. Outwardly, we are not the most impressive of nature's handiwork. Yet by the power of memory and imagination we made ourselves lords of the earth, and even that was not enough. Memory and imagination enabled us to conquer but also created a new need – not just to succeed but to understand. So we sought to penetrate the deepest secrets of existence, even though every instinct of self-preservation warned us to keep clear of such dangerous territory.

There is a universality about religion which is astounding. It has never been the prerogative of one class, race, sex or social condition. It has cut across natural and artificial distinctions, even moral ones, for it has inspired both innumerable acts of creative self-sacrifice and many awful crimes. There are grim, bloodstained pages in religion's book. It has sometimes been a destructive force in human life, engendering hatred, organising persecution and provoking wars. According to its critics, when religion is not encouraging strife it is acting as a drug which numbs the human conscience and fills the human brain with escapist fantasies. Its supporters are tyrannical fanatics or fawning hypocrites seeming to exist in one of two equally unhealthy states: possessed either by an acute fever or a dull habit. Religion causes human beings to be narrow, superstitious, full of hatred and fear. And so on and on.

These charges are true. There is bad and good religion just as there is good and bad science, art and politics; just as there are bad and good people. And it is bad religion that usually steals the headlines. Much of the popular argument about religion is conducted from the wrong assumptions. Religion is treated as something that simply exists and people must either be for it or against it. So the distinction is not made between religious activities which are right and those that are wrong, between religious assertions which are true and those that are false, between religious emotions that are rational and those which are vicious. It is impossible to justify religion as a whole; it is only what is valid in religion that can and ought to be defended.

The Roman poet Lucretius saw nothing in religion other than the appalling spectacle of mortals grovelling before their gods, yet

3

the verdict of history is against him. On balance, religion has raised human beings to a higher plane, inspired heroic ventures in philosophical and political thought, in music and art, exploration and discovery. It has spurred human beings on to smash down barriers and cross frontiers not only on the map but in the human mind. And not least it has added to the colour and excitement of life through festival and ceremony, ritual eating and drinking, dancing and singing.

It is unfashionable to speak well of religion these days. Yet as a matter of elementary justice, it needs to be pointed out again and again how impoverished human life would be if it were possible to wipe every vestige of religion off the face of the earth. It has encouraged humans to aspire to a satisfying view of existence as a whole, to be haunted by a vision of the divinely beautiful, to revere a moral ideal which towers above custom and convention. And it is not just the élite – the scholars and artists and saints – who have been touched by religion's magic. It has woven a spell over the minds of ordinary people who know little of theological ideas or ecclesiastical subtleties. The strange yet uplifting truths of religion have become the property of the humblest and simplest, just as surely as they sometimes by-pass the worldly-wise and sophisticated, working a transformation in social values – making the ordinary person feel extraordinary and the extraordinary person feel ordinary.

We use the term 'God' so often and in so many ways without realising what a remarkable idea it stands for. There is no other construct the human mind has achieved which can account for so much: nothing less than everything; existence as a whole, life, the world, human origins, history and destiny. All our knowledge, hopes and fears can be organised with reference to this one supreme principle. It is an elegant solution to the conundrum of existence; this idea of God as a self-existent being who unites me and my world, holds them in existence, and then finally determines our fate according to the divine will.

The God-idea transformed evolution by drawing struggling humanity towards those things that are excellent and beautiful and true. That's a generalisation vulnerable to those who point out that humanity has sometimes chosen brutal and destructive gods. But the remarkable thing is that when the term 'God' represents a degraded view of reality rather than an elevated one, we believe there has been a deviation from the norm. Human beings expect their gods to set them good examples.

These are just some of the things religion has meant for that little animal which back in the mists of the past chose a different path from its fellow creatures. And all that follows is a celebration of this central fact about the human species: that we are incurably religious.

1 THE MAKING OF MOO

Some years ago, the novelist Nigel Dennis wrote a play called *The Making of Moo*. It's about a British colonial officer in a remote part of Empire who discovers that in building a dam he has destroyed the river god Ega. The god died because the dam reduced to a trickling backwater the river on which the people's life depended. At first, simply as a game to pass the long tropical nights, the colonial officer and his wife discuss how they can create for the people another god to replace Ega. Stuck for a name, they hear the lowing of cattle in the distance and decide to call the new god Moo. They work out forms of worship, the wife writes a holy book, 'The Revelations of Moo', and they recruit one of the officers on the station who is musical to compose hymns and sacred songs to the new deity.

But what began as a joke becomes deadly serious. The worship of Moo develops a momentum all its own, before long involving bizarre rituals including blood sacrifice. The colonial officer appoints his native servant Pope and ends up killing as heretics any local people who still cling doggedly to he worship of the old god, Ega.

Over the years, the worship of Moo becomes the established religion of the region and is even carried by missionaries to remote places. And as is often the case, the theology of Mooism gets more sophisticated as time wears on. The barbaric practices of the early days give place to more civilised forms of religious observance. The founders of the new faith learn the game as they go along, and learn well. They realise that the old god Ega had died because he was a tangible object in the world, a river, something whose performance could be measured and found wanting. When the dam came, the river-bed dried up and there were no floods to irrigate the thirsty land, so the people felt let down by their god and turned their backs on him.

The founders of Mooism pondered the unhappy fate of Ega and laid down some theological principles to protect their deity. They declared Moo to be invisible; all statues and representations of him were outlawed. He retreated beyond the range of the telescope and measuring rod, let alone the unaided eyes of the people. Moo was worshipped as a pervasive spirit; everywhere and yet nowhere at once. The advantages were obvious. Because Moo was invisible, his existence could not be proved, so it became a matter of faith. But his existence couldn't be denied, either. He was invulnerable. No tribal witch doctor could rattle the bones at him and neutralise his magic. No advance in technology such as the building of a dam could rob him of his power.

Moo became a very adaptable deity. Whatever the founders of the faith decreed to be a sign of his presence was attributed to him, whereas happenings that brought misery or disaster on his people were blamed on some malevolent, destructive lesser god dedicated to Moo's overthrow. Once Moo became invisible, worship and theology turned into more complicated matters, shrouded in mystery. Because the ordinary people found the idea of an invisible god hard to get into their heads, they had to ask for help from cleverer people – the chosen few whom Moo appointed his chief servants and interpreters. A growth-industry of priests and theologians sprang up.

These scholars had little difficulty in proving that Moo, far from being a recent arrival amongst the pantheon of gods, had in fact been worshipped by the ancient Egyptians but under a more primitive name. And to show there was no conflict between science and religion, the theologians wrote learned papers demonstrating how in the beginning Moo inspired his followers to use modern technology in the form of dam-building to demolish false gods like Ega and reveal his own nature.

In honour of Moo, schools and hospitals and cathedrals were built and wealthy benefactors offered large cheques for their names to be associated with these institutions. As the state religion, Mooism enjoyed all the privileges of holiness such as tax exemption and high social status for its leaders.

But the worldly success of Mooism produced disillusionment amongst some of the purists of the faith, especially the founder's son, a fanatic who wanted to get back to the original religion, the strict letter of the holy Book of Moo – though he had no idea how it came to be written. He knew that his family were in at the very beginning when Moo first announced his presence amongst men, but he was unaware that Moo had actually been invented by his father around the supper table. Like a latter-day Luther, the founder's son demanded a Reformation. He longed to rediscover the pure, uncorrupted Gospel of Moo and set off with reforming zeal to trace Mooism back to its origins, ignoring his distraught mother's warning that he ought to leave well alone. The beginnings of Moo or of any god are best left shrouded in mystery.

There the play ends. It's a satire on Christianity, of course, but it makes some useful points about religion in general. How did Mooism qualify as a religion at all? To begin with, it was about personal faith. The people trusted Moo to succeed where Ega had failed. But it also had a body of beliefs – statements about who Moo was, what he had done and what he demanded of his followers. This is where theological doctrines and dogmas and the clever people who deal in such things entered the picture.

Mooism also had a social dimension – it was an organisation. People who roughly shared the same body of beliefs worshipped and prayed and met together. They celebrated the mighty deeds of Moo in sustaining the prosperity of the region and ensuring the river didn't dry up. This fellowship offered a mixture of authority, guidance, inspiration and human warmth to individuals who might otherwise feel out of things. And because Mooism was the state religion, it was in the organisational power-game, shaping culture and politics; its priests powerful figures in public as well as religious life. Lastly, there was Mooism as a code of ethics. Duties were laid down for the followers of the religion. Mooistic law as interpreted by the priests governed the way devotees behaved not only in their personal and family lives but at work and in public.

These are the distinguishing marks of most religions. They are about personal faith, a body of beliefs, a code of ethics and some form of organisation. There may be more than these four parts to a particular religion but there cannot be less if it is to do its job properly. The particular importance a religion gives to any of the four will vary greatly. Some religions are all action and very little theology. For others, such as Judaism and Islam, the Law counts above all else. Religions are moulded by such factors as the culture in which they arise or the temperament of the people or the old religions they have displaced. Mooism was fashioned in such a way as to make up for what was lacking in the discredited river god Ega.

This points to one of the interesting morals of the tale of Moo. When the river god Ega fails, the people aren't content to be happy atheists but thankfully transfer their allegiance to another god. Religions which collapse don't usually leave a vacuum. They are superseded, as was paganism by Christianity in Britain. All that remained of the ancient hymns and dances of Europe were absorbed into Christianity, the Winter Solstice became Christmas, the holy places of the new religion were thronged with devotees who handled bread and wine as once they had brandished mistletoe or kissed stone images of the horned god.

Theological argument and criticism amongst believers or intellectual attacks by sceptics never prove fatal to a religion. Gods rarely die in battle; they either expire from old age and feebleness or suffer accidental death – knocked down when they get in the way of humanity's forward movement. And on the whole, atheism is a hobby for intellectuals. The ordinary people are rarely atheists, perhaps because they live much too near the bone and need all the help they can get.

As the demise of Ega proved, gods can fail, especially if they are relied on so directly to meet material needs that fortuitous events like the drying up of a river-bed can expose their weaknesses. It seems sensible to create or adopt gods who can cope with the whole of our lives and not just one particular aspect of it. The Romans, whose organisational genius was reflected in their religion, had a god for every conceivable activity. In agriculture, for example, one god was responsible for ploughing, another for weeding and a third for harvesting. But what happened to them all? Or to those splendid Greek gods whose stories are amongst the greatest treasures of literature? Did they merely change their name and become aspects of the same reality Christians, Jews or Muslims worship as God? Perhaps gods perish when they can no longer adapt to change. Greek and Babylonian gods were nation-gods and when the state collapsed they crumbled as well. This is why the prophet Amos shrewdly insisted that Jehovah's existence must in no way be bound up with the fate of the Jewish state. However religions die, the gap is soon filled: the place religion occupies in the life of humanity is too important to be left vacant for long.

Arthur Koestler once edited a book called *The God that Failed*. In it, he and several other intellectuals describe how their original infatuation with Marxism was followed by growing disillusionment and final abandonment of the whole ideology. But whilst they were within the magic circle of belief, Marxism offered them all the elements of a true religion. They felt let down not by any of Marxism's shortcomings as a system of ideas but by its rigidity, its inability to change with the times. The moral seems to be that your chosen God mustn't be so firmly nailed to one set of circumstances that he or it can't make the jump to another.

Another lesson of *The Making of Moo* is that it is almost impossible to think up a new religion which is not a modification or adaptation of one that already exists – unless, of course, it is some crackpot notion which originates on the wilder shores of human eccentricity. There are those plots beloved of science-fiction writers where the deity is an outlandish machine or biological mutant, but in real life the pedigree of allegedly new religions can easily be traced. Mooism, for instance, was a crude imitation of Christianity which in its time parted company with Judaism, a religion that came out of the cultural melting pot of the Near East and before that emerged from primitive cults of totemism and clan worship. Islam has been described as Christianity's younger cousin and Buddhism began as a Hindu reform movement, and so on and on. I am not arguing here any evolutionary case that what came after must by definition be better or more advanced than what went before. I'm simply noting the fact hat the roots of most religions seem to drive deep down into the sub-soil of religions that came before them.

The Making of Moo implies that human beings can have genuine religious feelings about false gods. The people in Nigel Dennis's play who transferred their allegiance from Ega the river god to Moo were probably just as sincere in their worship of the new god as they had been in their allegiance to the old one. There is no necessary connection between the truth in a religion and its hold over people. This is why it is possible to invent religions.

Perhaps the most important lesson the playwright Nigel Dennis was trying to get across is that religion can be a dangerous force that we play around with at our peril. We may think we are manipulating religion's power to our advantage, but it can easily get out of control and wreak havoc in our lives. To take it for granted that religion must be a force for good is foolish; it is a conjecture which flies in the face of history and our own experience. There are spiritual powers abroad that inspire us to do things beyond our brightest hopes or awful things that exceed our most debased imaginings. Not the least of bad religion's malevolent powers is its uncanny way of pandering to our egotism and distorting our thinking. So we end up with a warped view of the relationship between ourselves and the universe, for we have been encouraged to remake reality in our own image.

All this belongs to that vague area where religion and superstition, magic and sorcery intersect. Religion has always had its forbidden territory which believers were taught to keep out of for their own safety. The priest and the magician have been at war almost from the dawn of history, the priest content to serve supernatural powers whilst the magician tried by spells and incantations to outwit these powers, bending them like yoked oxen to his will. Not for nothing did the early Church regard exorcism as an important branch of Christian service which purged religion of its unhealthy and destructive elements by striking at their roots in the human personality. On the whole, the modern Church leaves that sort of issue to the psychiatrists. Perhaps it is wrong to do so.

Was the cult of Moo religion or magic? Can any religion which is the product of human ingenuity, however idealistically conceived, avoid the taint of magic, the suspicion that we are going through the motions of religion not because a higher power commands or inspires us to, but because there's something in it for us? Throughout history, human beings have turned to religion to stave off disaster, conquer disease, reverse a cruel fate, win happiness, prosperity and long life. There's nothing wrong with that. But we live on a spiritual knife-edge between the desire to serve God, which is what true religion is about, and the attempt to get God to serve us, which is magic. We have been warned.

DIY RELIGION

Suppose I were to attempt my own version of *The Making of Moo* and start a new religion? How would I go about it? Starting from scratch usually involves beginning with a blank sheet of paper or a pile of bricks or an uncultivated patch of ground. What does it mean to start a religion from scratch? I am not labouring under the delusion I am some latter-day Buddha or Confucius or even a Mary Baker Eddy or Charles Taze Russell, the founder of the Jehovah's Witnesses. It could only be a game, but in fact it's more serious than that: let's call it an exercise in learning how religion works by trying to construct one from first principles.

For a start, I'd have to try to jump out of my own skin because I already have a religion. Starting all over again would mean wiping out all I was brought up to believe or learnt at school or have come to accept as my personal faith. It would be like attempting to recover my lost innocence – to think and act as though a thousand and one things had never happened to me. Christianity has made me what I am; it was bred into my bone and has formed my view of what life is all about; it has coloured my language and thoughts and influenced my actions. It would be cheating not to recognise that at the outset. So I must make full allowance for my in-built biases and try to ensure that I don't consciously fool myself or anyone else.

I am bound to draw most of my illustrations about religion from Christianity because it's the only faith of which I have any first-hand knowledge. However, though Christians, Jews and Muslims do things very differently, there are striking similarities between them – besides the obvious fact they appear to worship the same God under different names. As the jargon has it, believers have the same psychological profile; their aims are broadly similar; they think the same way even when the content of their thought is different. Their religious rites vary, but they are obviously performed for the same purpose.

This doesn't mean that the differences between Christians, Muslims and Jews are so small as to be unimportant or that all religions are equally true, but it does suggest that Judaism, Christianity and Islam seem to have grown out of the same sub-soil of what we can only call basic religion. What W. R. Inge, Dean of St Paul's in the 1920s, said about Christianity, 'The Gospel of Christ is not a religion, but religion itself in its universal and deepest significance'[1] would be echoed by Muslim or Jewish scholars – but speaking up for their own faith. They all believe theirs is the most faithful expression of true religion.

Social surveys over the past decades say that around seventy per cent of the British population claims to believe in God, though without feeling the urge to go looking for him in the nearest parish church, mosque or synagogue. The figure varies slightly from year to year but only within very narrow limits. Add this to the fact that basic religious sentiments are shared by believers such as Christians, Jews and Muslims, whose official beliefs divide them, and it's clear there's a lot of raw religion around – raw in the sense that it has no theological label and is common both to the developed faith of those who go to church or mosque and the vague religiosity of those who don't. It is this reservoir of raw religion on which I shall need to draw if my DIY project is to be a serious experiment in religious thinking rather than an exercise in personal eccentricity or just a silly game.

Trying to create a religion is like one of those experiments where students of electronics make a model of a living organ, the human brain, by getting a computer to duplicate its operations. The results thus far have fallen far short of the real thing; nevertheless, in the process, much is being learned about the way our brain works. But it's an artificial business. So is trying to make our own religion. We cannot command our feelings to fasten upon whatever deity our minds invent, any more than we could force ourselves to fall in love with a particular person to order. In a sense, that very fact may prevent the whole thing from degenerating into frivolity or absurdity. If whatever concept we evolve is obviously incapable of triggering our religious emotions, then what we are contemplating is strictly unbelievable and we know we are up against a dead end.

Why would one want to go in for DIY religion? Certainly DIY is a booming industry in our society, and not just for activities such as assembling furniture or putting in a new bathroom. There's DIY education called home-learning and DIY politics. This is how one spokesman described his party recently: no party line imposed from above; no national leader to call the tune; so long as you are kind to the environment, you can cobble together policies which are tailor-made for your own community. So the notion of DIY religion isn't all that bizarre.

How does DIY meet our needs? There may be a gap in the market which none of the large suppliers is filling. Their product doesn't exactly fit our requirements, perhaps because it hasn't kept up with the times. That applies to religions too. Most of the great religions such as Christianity or Islam emerged a long time ago in far-away places when people thought the earth was flat, evil spirits caused diseases and the rest of the planets revolved around ours. Why squeeze back into the thought-world of Jesus or Muhammad or Moses? Surely it's possible to evolve a religion that takes account of global warming, nuclear fission, television and modern democracy?

Or we are sometimes driven to DIY because the retailers have got too big, too remote and too expensive. They're run by professionals, accountants whose first concern seems to be profits or managers who want to produce what suits *them* rather than us. They claim to know what's best for us but often they don't, which is why so many companies go bust.

Religions, too, can get too big, too remote and too expensive; run by professionals – priests and theologians – who seem to be in a different world from ourselves and whose main preoccupation is to keep the company afloat rather than to supply our needs. I don't need to labour the point. The shelves of religious bookshops groan under the weight of books bemoaning what is called the irrelevance of the Church.

Perhaps the strongest possible reason for DIY is the personal satisfaction that comes from creating something which is our own in a very special way. It has taken our time, commitment and skill, and the result is moulded to fit exactly our living space. We want a religion which fits our personalities – indeed, there's not much point in one that doesn't. The good life is hard enough to achieve without the additional handicap of obeying religious laws evolved in a far-away time or a strange culture.

One of the least lovable characters of our time, Adolf Hitler, decided to invent a religion which perfectly met his needs and served his purposes. He did a massive DIY job by marrying the old Nordic tribal gods to a perversion of Christianity and turned Nazism into a religion with a single-sentence creed, 'There is no God but Germany.' He employed all the paraphernalia of religion ranging from a sacred book, *Mein Kampf*, to mass rallies with stirring music, a wealth of symbol and ritual, much of it to do with blood sacrifice. And at its heart was an oath of absolute loyalty to the Messiah, the Führer. Tragically, he had no difficulty in recruiting millions of true believers – which says something about the power of the religious impulse even when it is grotesquely distorted.

At the other end of the scale, there are any number of invented religions that attract only the minimum membership – which is one. You don't have to get the raw material of DIY from a large store. You can make do with bits and pieces that lie close at hand, which are your own very personal property. The philosopher Alfred North Whitehead said that religion is what we do with our solitariness – for him it was about winning meaning and purpose for our own lives before it had anything to do with those religious activities people practise together.

Find the source of our religion within ourselves? That sounds like an act of monstrous egotism, and yet if we are trying to visualise a personal God what higher examples of personality are known to us than human ones? We must measure everything by our own experience because that is our only yardstick. When we cast around for ways of describing God, human images are the best we can do – we describe God as King or Father or Shepherd or Lord. We know perfectly well that these are only metaphors or analogies, and we understand their limits; for example, we don't believe for a moment that God the Father procreates children in the same way as a human parent. But even Jesus couldn't find a higher image than fatherhood to convey the nature of God to those he taught.

It's safe to say, then, that one source of DIY religion is staring me right in the face every time I shave. Just like a DIY enthusiast finding under his nose at home materials he thought he would have to get elsewhere, so there are qualities within me which are an essential element in any religion worth the name – as I shall hope to show.

Of course, we don't have to build our DIY structure from raw timber, we can join together bits and pieces of old furniture that happen to be lying around. When it is religion rather than wardrobes we are talking about, the technical term for a patchwork of gods is polytheism, one of the oldest and most widespread forms of belief. If one God equals one majestic truth which draws our life together and commands our utter loyalty, then many of us would have to own up to a streak of polytheism. Beneath our calm exteriors we are a warring mass of conflicting aims, a veritable zoo of squabbling instincts; we are driven hither and thither by a swirl of hopes and fears, truths and lies. We can worship a whole galaxy of deities, not just hanging on to this truth at one moment and that truth at another, but acknowledging a number of so-called truths at the same time – like those rows of altars by the roadside along which honest polytheists filed to pay their tributes, one after the other.

Is Mars, the god of war, dead in our lives, or Bacchus, the god of drunken conviviality, or the seductive Venus, or Mercury, the god of crafty diplomacy or Mammon, whose splendid temples dominate the financial centres of the world? Money, power, sex, ambition, success, happiness: we don't call them gods of course, but they have the influence and command the devotion which has traditionally belonged to the Deity.

But even this early on, I must rule out polytheism as a personal option. I'm not well enough organised to cope with a view of reality split into any number of divine parts. I realise the importance of polytheism as a civilising force in cultures such as ancient Greece and Rome, but I don't really understand how human beings came to divide up into many parts a religious experience whose impact they must originally have felt as a unity. The human mind, especially the western variety, tends to unite and reconcile things rather than to divide and react to them separately. So, with all respect to religions such as Hinduism, polytheism is not for me.

But we have plenty of deities to choose from if we decide to go for ready-made rather than bespoke religion. The early Greek scientist, Thales, complained that his world was full of gods. It still is, whatever conclusions the experts draw from statistics about the decline in churchgoing and religious belief. Gods are being made and unmade all over the place.

And there's an element of DIY in all religion, even in the great traditional faiths whose essential structures have been fixed for centuries. They seem to loom out of the mists of the past like great mountain ranges – apparently there since time began – yet some of their founders were accused of the precise offence of indulging in DIY. The scribes and Pharisees in first-century Palestine couldn't make up their minds whether Jesus of Nazareth was taking over the old religion or starting a new one. He was accused of doing both.

If you were to question closely a hundred members of a religious congregation who claim to worship the same God according to the rites and doctrines of a particular sect or denomination, you would find a hundred subtly different expressions of that faith. The only God any of us can really know is our own God; we don't know what goes on in the deepest recesses of our neighbours' hearts and can only take their word for what their God is like. We have to take it on trust that we are worshipping the same God when we kneel together.

We might claim, for example, to be Christians – by which we mean we identify with the doctrines and ethos of Christianity – but there may be certain clauses of the creeds we say with our fingers crossed or privately hold doctrines officially condemned as heresies. Our general identification with Christianity is close enough for other insiders to recognise us as card-carrying believers, but our private faith reflects the fact that we are unique personalities and we put our own distinctive stamp on our religion. Mother Teresa and Billy Graham share a common world-view, as did John Knox and St Francis, C. H. Spurgeon and Cardinal Newman, Albert Schweitzer and Archbishop William Temple, but the proverbial man from Mars might find that hard to believe observing the diversity in their worship, doctrine and life styles.

Beliefs and personalities tend to fit one another like hand and glove, especially in an age of individualism such as ours. It is one of the key characteristics of our time that there is a greater element of choice in many things, including religion. People no longer automatically take on the religious beliefs of their parents or their culture. Even though we call modern western society secular, in this sense at least it is a more religious age than previous ones. Religion does not have to be an inheritance or a habitual pattern of behaviour; it is a more conscious option than in former times – not just the choice between one religion and another but between any religion and none.

In most religions, there is a great gap between official teaching and the doctrines ordinary believers privately hold to. Even in the so-called Ages of Faith such as medieval times, the secret beliefs of the ordinary people were often a strange amalgam of orthodox Christianity and old pagan practices including sorcery, witchcraft and fertility rites drawn from Europe's pre-Christian past. People of most cultures and every age have chosen from the religious ideas available to them those they thought would aid their survival and enrich their lives. Students of Chinese religion often say that though there used to be three official religions in pre-revolutionary China – Confucianism, Taoism and Buddhism – in some strange way, many Chinese seemed able to belong to all three at once, choosing bits of this one and that to meet their needs.

In real life, religions rarely fit into neat, clearly defined pigeon-holes. I learned this lesson when I first went to Central Africa as a missionary and was taken to the funeral of a tribal chief in the Zambezi Valley. After he had received a Christian burial, his wives performed over his body rites that harked back to the tribe's pre-Christian religious past. When I expostulated to a wise old African minister that at the very least the two burial ceremonies involved a clash of contradictory ideas, he gently made it clear that

I was the victim of a western either–or mentality, whereas the African mind can hold together incompatible ideas without trying to resolve the contradictions in them. In this sense, he hinted, even tribal Africans live in a much more complex thought-world than that of the problem-solving westerner for whom something is either one thing or the other. Many traditional Africans will draw on Christianity and animism and ancestor-worship at critical moments in their lives without any sense of incongruity, selecting those elements likely to help them get through.

Western society is said to be thoroughly secular and it has certainly liberated itself from Christendom, yet it is riddled with every conceivable form of religiosity. People are suckers for Sufis, zipped out on Zen, mad about the mantras, gone on gurus, awed by astrology and eerie about exorcism. We privately draw our spiritual inspiration from a vast reservoir of religious and pseudo-religious notions – as the man said who missed an airliner that crashed, 'As luck would have it, fate was on my side, thank God!'

We can see how DIY faith relates to the party line by noting the way splits and divisions often come about. Our private beliefs can coexist quite happily with orthodox religious doctrine within certain limits, but the problems really start when our divergences from orthodoxy become so sharp that we can no longer go on adapting it to our own needs. Then the DIY element takes over. We may think that the Church is too old-fashioned for our taste, or, on the other hand, that it seems so determined to be with-it that it neglects elements of the traditional faith which we personally regard as essential. Thus the early Protestants felt that the religious Establishment was elevating the Church above the Bible and so neglecting the Word of God. The result was a splintering of Christianity.

Another way the DIY element of religion may take over is when someone believes himself or herself, rightly or wrongly, to be the recipient of a new truth from God, and this may be an idea the traditional faith cannot or will not accommodate. So Mary Baker Eddy broke away from US Congregationalism to found Christian Science out of the conviction that the material world, including its diseases, is an illusion which can be countered by spiritual control.

Insights such as these may be true or false but there is usually no difficulty in finding people to believe in them.

So there's an honourable tradition of DIY in religion. But it does raise one big question. The issue was put starkly by the prophet Micah. He warned, 'You must not worship things you have made yourself' (Mic. 5:13). It is the sin picturesquely described in the Bible as 'whoring after false gods'. Isn't that what we'd be doing in inventing our own religion?

3 THE REAL THING?

'Invent your own God? That would be idolatry!' some people might protest, scandalised. Strictly, I'm about the business of inventing my own religion which is not the same thing as inventing a God. I'm concerned with the journey, not the destination. I can get to Manchester via a route used by so many people that a motorway has been built to accommodate them or I can strike off across country, choosing my own route. I may or may not reach Manchester that way, but if there is any originality in what I am doing, it is in inventing the journey; I don't imagine for a moment that I'm also inventing the destination.

Of course, I may not even know for sure that Manchester exists. I have heard rumours of a great city way beyond our parish boundaries, I've met people who claim to have walked its streets, and my common sense tells me there ought to be somewhere like it. Like the early explorers seeking El Dorado or the New World, I must mark out my route and set off in faith.

Nevertheless, I am in dangerous territory. The possibility of idolatry is always there, for unless I have some idea of God in my mind, how do I know what my religion ought to consist of? So what about the perils of idolatry? Religions such as Hinduism have no problem, but I've already ruled that out as a model – my western mind cannot cope with such religious complexity. On the other hand, Judaism, Christianity and Islam regard idolatry with abhorrence. The Hebrew words translated as 'idol' in the Authorised Version of the Bible, mean 'object of terror', 'thing of nought', 'abominable' and 'cause of grief'. And in the New Testament, idolaters are consigned to the less than admirable company of liars, dogs, extortioners and adulterers.

And yet . . . how can a human being whose main contact with the world is through his senses avoid giving some shape and form to whatever he comes to believe in? A verse of Hindu Scripture says, 'Thou art formless. Thy only form is our knowledge of thee.' As soon as we grasp either through our five senses or a special sixth sense the nature of reality, we have created an idol, even if it is only a theological idea. Yet without it we would be adrift without a compass in an endless ocean.

Every religion that claims to offer God to human beings is, by definition, idolatrous because it has been evolved by people – an Ism or Anity or Ology which is the product of human ingenuity, one of any number of attempts throughout history to make sense of Whoever or Whatever triggers our religious feelings. Even those who believe that religion begins with a divine initiative, that God makes the first move, don't claim that this God of revelation reveals a religion; they say he reveals himself.

We have no other choice than to be idolaters if we wish to get our minds round a reality that is strictly beyond human comprehension. In one Old Testament incident, God refuses to allow human beings to pin a label on him: 'Call me "I will be what I will be"'; yet in another, he is described as 'the God of Abraham, Isaac and Jacob'. The pure essence of eternal reality is already being distilled into earthen vessels. God's being was not bounded by the imagination, obedience and spiritual insight of the Patriarchs, but their humanity set limits on any ability to mediate him.

The Jews proclaimed their loathing of any pictorial representations of God – no graven images, they declared. Yet human nature and the character of human language defeated them. No laws could forbid the making of mental pictures. Hence, in the very same Scriptures that contain the stern prohibition on idolatry, God is described as walking in the Garden of Eden, he stretches out his arm, his voice shakes the cedars, he can be tasted and found good. To forbid the making of pictures about God would be to rule out any thoughts of him at all, for we are so made that we can only think in pictures.

Because we are human, we are riddled with contradictions and absurdities, muddled in our thinking and emotionally mixed-up. To believe that any understanding of God which is within our comprehension is *not* idolatrous but is the Truth with a capital T – fixed, final and beyond argument – is a dangerous illusion. It might also be the subtlest form of idolatry, practised by those who insist their image of God may be a miniature but is a true likeness and certified as such by the subject himself.

It's hard to imagine that people ever set out deliberately to manufacture a God. More likely, having seen some reason to believe in a God of sorts, they proceed to make the best likeness they can from materials available to them. Scholars argue about the origins and development of religion. How could anyone know? Something like this might have happened. Humanity started off by venerating material objects such as oddly shaped stones, then they lifted their sights to great natural features of their world such as the planets, rivers, mountains and the sea, and then they turned to the world as an abstract reality, as the sum of everything which makes up their life and thoughts, hopes, dreams and fears. And then they fell into the hands of the theologians and philosophers.

It's hard to see how humanity on its long journey through time could have avoided idolatry, though, in an attempt to dodge the trap, some great religious thinkers have chosen the negative path – endless descriptions of what God *is not*. This way they don't have to describe him positively and so create a picture that is bound to be idolatrous. Here is an extract from an early work called *Mystical Theology*: '[God is not] soul or mind or imagination or reason or understanding . . . not number or order or greatness or littleness or equality or inequality . . . not immovable or at rest . . . nor darkness nor light nor error nor truth . . .'

Such a description may get round the problem of idolatry, but at what price? Who precisely would one be praying to or believing in? It may be idolatry to say that God is something, yet it is linguistic nonsense to say that he is nothing; otherwise, what need have we for the term 'god'? It's a pretty poor definition of anything to say that it's not something else. If that's all we can say about it, then unless we know what the other thing is, we can't say anything about it at all. Most ordinary people might feel it worth indulging in a bout of honest idolatry in order to avoid that kind of logic.

Does anyone really worship an idol? They may worship God in the form of an idol, but that is a different thing. According to Bishop Heber's hymn, the 'heathen in his blindness bows down to wood and stone'. Surely, someone who genuinely believes that a lump of stone in itself has supernatural powers is likely to discover sooner or later that he is mistaken, that the stone's power comes through something beyond itself. Certainly, Bishop Heber's 'heathen' could worship God in the form of an idol because that's what idols are for – to concentrate the mind and spirit, and to locate divine power in a special place, person or thing. But there's all the difference in the world between a statue and a conviction – what something is in itself and what it prompts us to believe.

Commenting on cow-worship in Hinduism, George Cantwell Smith wrote, 'The Hindu reveres the cow that he sees, not the cow that we see.'[2] As outsiders, we merely see a four-legged beast; the Hindu sees much more in and beyond it. Fundamentalist Christians claim that the Bible *is* the Word of God, every dot and comma of it, whilst other Christians insist that such a view turns the Bible into an idol and it is better to say that the Bible *contains* the Word of God. In itself, it is nothing other than a compendium of the history and literature of the Judaeo-Christian religion, and to regard it with undue veneration is idolatry.

Jesus was alive to this problem, which is why according to the fourth gospel, he warned his disciples, 'He who believes in me does not believe in me but in him who sent me' (John 12:44). He was aware that the bearer of the Ultimate might be confused with the Ultimate itself, which is what has happened throughout Christian history. The Jesus-People of the Swinging Sixties are a modern example. Jesus was their idol, just as ten years before it had been Che Guevara and ten years later Bob Dylan. They wanted to brush aside twenty centuries of Christian history and countless generations of the Jewish past and cherish a Jesus without either forebears or posterity. They chose Christ without Christianity – an idol, in fact, though one which inspired many of them to joyous, spontaneous living and a rejection of the tawdry materialism of their culture. Can there be anything vicious or evil in Jesusolatry, however superficial and narrow a religion it might be?

My point is simply that no human concept of God can ever be final, fixed and inerrant. Christians insist that Jesus Christ is the final revelation of God. Now the fact may be final but any dogma based on it cannot be: it is a human construct and so partial. It therefore behoves Christians to be cautious in the judgments they make about other religions. They may claim that Christ was Very God of Very God because they insist they are speaking from experience. But to go on from there and draw the conclusion that therefore Krishna, say, is a false God, is to make an assumption without evidence. How could they possibly know? All believers who express their understanding of God in theological language should think twice before they accuse others of idolatry.

Every change in our concept of God to keep step with our moral evolution leaves behind an idol. Once our gods lag behind our civilised progress, they can no longer be believed in. Were I to propose that the religion I intended to create demanded child-sacrifice or even the disembowelling of kittens, I might be physically assaulted in the supermarket or hauled into court by the RSPCA. Public opinion would not tolerate veneration of a deity out of step with current moral standards. Nor would it occur to me to disembowel a kitten on the off-chance the act might put me in touch with divinity. It's not an option open to me, not because it is theologically unthinkable – stranger things than this have been proposed by great religious minds in the past – but because it is morally repugnant. Any God who will only make himself known to me if I offer him a suffering animal is my moral inferior and therefore a discredited divinity. I may be an idolater but my chosen gods have got to do better than that.

With great realism, the Old Testament recognises all this and insists that the distinction between true and false gods is not a matter of theological argument but of practical evidence. The prophets invite those who follow gods other than Jehovah to a trial of strength. Divinity is as divinity does. The true God is the one who keeps his promises, who can out-perform his rivals. In the most matter-of-fact way, the Bible assumes that all people are religious. They may for various reasons change their gods, and the true God is the one who stands up to the severest practical examination.

This is a minefield and I do well to tread with care. I am unlikely to go whoring after false gods in the sense of bizarre idols; the greater danger is that I could become hopelessly trapped in a world of illusion. If through my DIY project I create any idols, they are more likely to be flights of fancy than anything else. Plato was alive to this danger, which is why he defined religion as an instinct for reality. That certainly sets boundaries to any experiment in DIY religion. I've got to be realistic. If I once lose touch with reality, the game is up. I would be in *Alice in Wonderland* territory, which may be an utterly delightful place to visit but cannot be a place of permanent residence for those who do not enjoy the luxury of living wholly within their imaginations.

The test of reality applies to every human activity. To build a house in defiance of the law of gravity is a certain recipe for disaster; to rewire a kitchen and play fast and loose with the laws of electricity is suicidal folly. To fashion a roof-beam of balsa wood because it's easier to carve, or water down cement in order to make it go further, is to fly in the face of reality. Good DIY depends on staying in close contact with reality. So does religion, which has this dangerous power to heat the blood, inflame the mind and conjure into existence weird phantoms we think are gods, until the fever passes and in the cold light of reality we see we have been duped.

Questions of truth or falsity in religion must be taken seriously because, according to the dictionary, truth means correspondence with reality, and, though an illusion may seem to work for a while, sooner or later it will collapse under the dead-weight of incontro-vertible facts which it can't cope with. Truth can cope with any facts; they may be challenging and uncomfortable, but of its nature truth is capable, however painfully, of expanding to accommodate them.

Most of the elaborate intellectual hoaxes perpetrated on hu-manity in the guise of political and religious philosophies sooner or later collapse under the impact of some truth they are no longer able to resist. Truth is a sort of map of reality we tamper with at our peril. That's what happened in Stalinist Russia; the ideologues tried to bend reality to fit their understanding of it. Street maps were redrawn to exclude all evidences of religion. Every place of worship was wiped off the maps; visitors could see great churches in front of their eyes but find no reference to them on the map in their hands.

Only a fool tampers with reality, because in the end it's the one thing that can be trusted. We may be forced to redraw our maps as new perceptions of reality strike us, but to do it the other way round and try to make reality fit our maps is madness.

How do I try to see that my religion stays in touch with reality? What is the difference between something being real and unreal? For example, I may be frightened out of my wits by what I thought was a ghost but which turns out to be someone covered in a white sheet. To state the obvious, we can only *think* that things are unreal; nothing can be unreal in itself. That ghost was just a chap in a white sheet – the unreality came in because I thought it was something else. The unreality was in me, not in the outside world. That's why Jesus said, 'First cast the beam out of your own eye' (Matt. 7:5).

How do we ever learn that something is unreal? Quite simply, we recall that we have been fooled in the past so we learn to examine carefully what we think is real in case it isn't. I'm less likely to be taken in the next time I visit a so-called haunted house and am confronted with a figure in a white sheet.[3] I also benefit from other people's experience. They don't all believe what I believe; they may think, for example, that ghosts don't exist whilst I think they do. They could persuade me to their way of thinking or I may get them to see things my way. But out of such differences of opinion we learn that there is unreality about.

But the most important way we guard against unreality is to put what we believe to be real to a practical test. The chap in the white sheet will go on deceiving people until someone is brave enough to grab him and reveal the hoax. False beliefs can only finally be discovered to be unreal when we try to live by them in daily life. Like phoney watches, they will be exposed because they don't do what they are supposed to do.

As with alleged ghosts, so too with religion. I must constantly be on my guard against unreality by remembering my own experience – the false gods I have worshipped, the erroneous ideas I pinned my hopes on, the trust I placed in things that cannot save – the unreality in me. I must also compare my thinking and experience with that of others engaged in the religious search. Vigorous argument often uncovers unreality, which is why heated theological controversy never does the Church any harm in the long run, whereas dull and unthinking conformity puts it in mortal danger. And I must put my model to the test. As the sceptical observer says to the DIY enthusiast who proudly displays his handiwork, 'It looks fine, but does it work?'

We may see a ghost because our imagination has run away with us. Our imagination paints mental pictures of the world; its raw material is anything our senses can pick up. And it can easily get at odds with our intellect. It may have been my imagination which led me to think the chap in the white sheet was a ghost whilst my mind was quietly trying to point out there was a laundry mark on the sheet. Or my intellect gives me good reasons why I ought not to drink because I'm driving, but my imagination projects on to the screen of my mind a foaming glass of cool beer on a hot day and my good intentions go out of the window or, more strictly, down my gullet.

So straight thinking is essential to hold our imagination in check or we'll soon be in the realms of fantasy. We may end up dealing with a reality so mind-blowing that the intellect is left far behind. But it is one thing for the intellect to cry, 'This is beyond me!'; quite another for it to snort, 'This is nonsense!' If it says that, then my invented religion is utterly futile, for what use is a God who is dimmer or dafter than I am?

The key truth or error question about any religion is this: is it simply the product of human ingenuity or does it involve a response to Something or Someone that transcends it? To put it in DIY terms – if I'm very clever I could make a television set that works splendidly from my end, the screen lights up, there's a healthy hiss of sound, but what kind of pictures appear on the screen or whether any do at all is outside my control. That's decided elsewhere, perhaps by the BBC and ITV, unless I'm only interested in transmitting through my set video pictures I've taken myself. But that novelty soon palls. In the same way, religions with a total membership of one are not only very restricted but awfully boring.

4

THE NEED FOR
A SUITCASE

DIY begins with some raw material and we
build from there, but before we choose the most
appropriate material for our task, we must
decide precisely what need our DIY gadget will
fulfil. We want extra accommodation in a small house or a garage
for our car or a swimming pool or perhaps a more modern kitchen.
DIY begins with the expression of a need. So does our religion.

The lesson of history seems to be that people have been religious
because they needed to be, so we ought to look first at the human
cravings which have best been met by whatever we call our God.
All life revolves around desire, and there have been no human
desires that have not looked to religion to satisfy them. Prayer
proves that: there is nothing humans could desire in life which has
not formed the basis of somebody's prayers.

Among the basic human desires are those to do with food, shelter
and security. The hunter's earliest religious practices were concerned with the animals on whom his survival depended, just as
rain-gods figured in the pantheon of cultivators who had a life-or-
death reliance on the seasons, and so on. Religious impulses of this
sort have the strongest hold on us when we are most dependent on
the forces of nature.

Over and over again in all kinds of ways, religion seems to bring
into focus the mingled motives and cravings of an unfulfilled life.
The range of possible human desires is shown by the differing ideas
of God held by human beings generally or perhaps by one human
being at different times. God may be creator, provider, source of

security and strength, or cosmic perfection to be worshipped 'in the beauty of holiness'. Whatever our need, there is a conception of the Deity which answers it. To compensate for our impotence, he is power; in our ignorance, he is omniscience; he meets our burdened consciences as Redeemer; for our guidance he is Holy Spirit. In some Hindu sects, initiates are assigned by their teacher a private name for God which reflects the guru's estimate of their basic need.

Fear is an important element in the human psyche. Our lives are bracketed between two oblivions and haunted by fear – of enemies, of nature, of sickness, of loneliness, and supremely, of death, for of all the creatures on earth, we alone know that we must die. Indeed, our experience teaches us to divide the world into safe and danger-ous zones, and out of this consciousness of peril much religion evolves.

In particular, death changes everything in basic societies, and not just for its victims – the handing on of property, the welfare of widows, the care of orphans and questions of clan succession affect the living, but so does the burial place of the dead and the condition of their spirits. Hence, a whole elaborate series of rites and rituals marks death and its aftermath. We need to know the dead are safe and that those on whom we depend will perform the rites necessary to secure our safety when we die.

We demand reassurance to assuage our insecurities. A well-known Welsh hymn would, if a few words were changed, express the basic supplication of many religions:

> Guide me, O thou great Jehovah,
> Pilgrim through this barren land;
> I am weak, but thou art mighty,
> Hold me with thy powerful hand.

Because human beings are thinking animals they also have a thirst for explanation. We do not merely experience, we reflect; we don't just endure, but hope. And we ask insistently, 'Why? How did it all begin? Where will it all end? Who am I? What is life all about?' From the beginning, humanity has lived in the information gulf between what our senses tell us and what out experience demon-strates we need to know in order to survive and be happy. We are driven to make the attempt to formulate theories of what the world is about.

Two questions in particular have wrestled the human mind to a standstill – the purpose of creation and the fact and meaning of evil. What has been called cosmological wonder is probably one of the commonest origins of religious thinking. 'Where were you when I laid the foundations of the world?' God asked Job (Job 38:4). The progressive enlargement of the little circle of light which symbolises human knowledge of the universe has revealed starkly the ever-expanding darkness beyond its boundary. How did nothing turn into something – indeed, into the glorious and terrible Everything we call the universe? That remains a question which religion has from time immemorial addressed.

Evil too has long baffled the thoughtful. The senselessness of undeserved suffering, the terrible destructiveness of natural calamity, the vicious ingenuity of human wickedness, and even more perplexing, the realisation that it is not just our worst intentions but the outworkings of our best efforts which can do great harm to ourselves and others – what of such awful realities? It is left to religion to make sense of this moral bedlam: both to offer an explanation of the ambiguities, perplexities and paradoxes of human existence and to provide the rituals by which their destructive effects can be countered.

Religion answers the human hunger for explanation by ascribing a meaning to life that may go far beyond the available evidence, and so is a matter of faith, but it seems to *work* for those who accept it as a source of inspiration and a means of support. When people say, 'I don't know what I would do without my religion', they presumably mean that it offers them a roughly satisfying way of explaining the otherwise inexplicable, giving them the confidence that everything will be all right in the end, and the strength to soldier on.

There is also something else at work in us – not so much a specific appetite like the desire for food or drink or friendship or knowledge or sex, but a vague longing. To be human is to have a feeling of dissatisfaction with our existence as it is, an almost indignant sense that there has got to be something more which is better than anything we presently possess.

Where does this vague ache come from? If we take evolution

seriously, all our aptitudes developed because there was a practical purpose for them. There were good reasons to do with survival and fulfilment why our forebears learned to walk upright or developed hands as multi-purpose tools. It's a common-sense assumption that the existence of a human faculty implies something for it to work on – a gnawing feeling in my gut presumes the possibility of food; a parched mouth requires the existence of moisture.

This strange longing to push beyond the frontiers of our present existence suggests there is something somewhere that can satisfy it. Some religions hold that whatever is capable of satisfying that longing comes from within us, but others believe that what is capable of assuaging this yearning and giving us peace has its source beyond ourselves. That is the dividing line between religions.

These, then, are the needs that our religion must satisfy. This is why we have embarked on a DIY project. But what sort of thing is it that fits the bill? That's the question a DIY enthusiast asks himself. What will do the job best? What is religion and how can it meet my deepest needs?

We looked at Mooism and decided what religion is constructed of – personal faith, a code of ethics, a set of beliefs and some form of organisation – but when you put them all together, what have you got? It sounds a very sloppy way of deciding this issue, but one must conclude that religion is about whatever people think is religious. Throughout history human beings have worshipped things, people and ideas both elevated and trivial, splendid and silly, predictable and amazing – but in every case, supremely important to them. Unlike the earth's atmosphere, the religious realm does not impose itself on us, revealing its presence by unmistakable signs such as howling gales, burning heat or showers of rain. For all we know, we may, in sheer ignorance, be moving around in worlds unseen, living in a spiritual environment as unconsciously as fish occupy water. Unless we show some interest in finding out, we'll be none the wiser. Ancient mariners never discovered there was a whole new world over the horizon until they summoned the courage and curiosity to push out beyond the limits of their sight.

Religion is a word that resists definition. But so do many other words that mean something to us. There are realities which defy definition just as there are definitions devoid of reality. What does 'yellow' mean? Religion is really a suitcase-word like 'sport'. What is sport? Bull-fighting may be a sport to you but not to many animal-lovers. You could draw up a list of all the activities people regard as sports and you are bound to leave some out. Or there's language. People don't speak language in general but specific languages such as French or German or Hindustani. Any definition of language must incorporate every conceivable form of communication between human beings. The list is endless and impossible to restrict; we just have to accept that a language is whatever makes contact possible between living creatures.

In fact, the notion of religion as a suitcase-word is apt, for one derivation of the term 'religion' means whatever binds everything together. Religion can't be excluded from our thinking because it's the very frame round our thinking. It would be like packing a suitcase and leaving out the case. Whether we like it or not, we have a general view of existence which colours everything we say and do. And that's our religion.

So our essential piece of equipment for this exercise in DIY religion is an interest in, a curiosity about, and, most important of all, an enthusiasm for whatever strikes us as evidence of religion. Enthusiasm is important because it's hard to see the point of a belief that fails to move us, which tickles our mind but is no spur to our spirits.

We shall need another quality too: courage. We can do nothing creative without taking risks. Every significant human activity involves courage because we are reaching towards some goal which is not within our grasp and might never be. The risk may be physical, emotional or moral as we put ourselves within range of harm or danger. No faith is beyond challenge, no belief so credible it is immune from attack, no conviction exempt from continual jeopardy. Much of faith's value depends on the element of hazard in it. So we need courage.

And in exploring the field of religion, we cannot afford to be too choosy either about our companions or the nooks and crannies we explore. Because human nature is an admixture of good and bad, we are bound to come across both good and bad religion, for the moral calibre of people and their religion are inextricably linked. St Francis of Assisi and the Pope who tried to silence him were both religious men. The Inquisitor who wielded the white-hot iron and the poor wretch to whom he applied it were equally devout. Religion includes both high mass at Westminster Cathedral and yoga exercises in a New Age commune. It is found in the Benedictine monastery and the Navaho Indian sweat lodge. We must be cautious at this stage in our prejudgments about what is proper religion and what is mere crankery – after all, Jesus and many of his most illustrious followers were in their time dismissed as lunatics.

Some religious truths only crystallise in our minds as we wrestled with the fact we cannot accept the so-called religious truths of others. 'That I can't believe!' may not be a very elevated sentiment but it is occasionally the beginning of wisdom. There are truths that would never have occurred to us but for the intuitions of the prophets, poets and mystics; there are other truths which arise as a by-product of our rejection of other people's bigotry and dogmatism.

We must not brush aside anyone who has given religion serious attention, even if we believe him or her to be mistaken. We may think someone of strong religious opinions is utterly wrongheaded, but who can doubt that these opinions are probably more important than anything else to him, beliefs to which he has clung through thick and thin, in good times and ill? Odd that in our time we pay close attention to other people's opinions about specific political or economic issues but think their view of everything – their religion – is either a private matter or largely irrelevant. What makes up a philosophy of life is considered much too vague and general to be contentious. Yet a dinner-party guest who announces that he thinks life is not worth living is a highly dangerous man, to be given a wide berth. If he means what he says, he's hardly likely to push you out of the way if he notices a chandelier falling from the ceiling on to your head nor will he draw the host's attention to the fact the mushrooms on the table are actually toadstools.

'The most practical and important thing about someone in his view of the universe,' wrote G. K. Chesterton. 'We think the question is not whether someone's theory of the cosmos affects matters but whether, in the long run, anything else affects them.'[4]

So, to paraphrase W. B. Yeats, in matters of religion we must tread softly lest we tread on other people's dreams.

It is worth recalling in the five hundredth anniversary year of Christopher Columbus's epic voyage to the New World that, as Carl Jung put it, 'Using subjective assumptions, a false hypothesis, and a route abandoned by modern navigation, Columbus nevertheless discovered America.'[5] We do well to think twice before we claim that our way is *the* way or that someone else's way is a dead-end.

5 BUILDING

REGULATIONS

I can't build what I like where and how I like. All kinds of regulations govern those DIY projects which involve sizeable construction tasks. And these building regulations are of two kinds, there are those which someone has laid down for reasons of safety or hygiene or environmental soundness. There are others which are built into the nature of the world and of the materials I am using. These are unalterable. The difference is easily illustrated. There could be the law that murder is punishable by death – that law Parliament could and did alter by ruling that capital punishment is not something a civilised society ought to countenance. But there could also be a law which says that to put your finger in an electric light socket is punishable by death. That is now a law Parliament could change except by banning electricity. It is not based on Parliament's opinion about civilised behaviour but on the observed facts of nature. Generally speaking, whenever people put their fingers in electric light sockets, they die.

These general laws of nature say that if you do one thing, another will follow as a matter of course; they don't depend on human opinion or consent. If you jump from a building you will hit the ground, the one thing is a necessary consequence of the other. On the other hand, if as a British subject you are already married and go through another marriage ceremony, you will go to jail. There's no necessary link between the two things; western society has simply decreed that there should be a link between marrying more than one wife and going to jail. If, however, you lived in a country governed by the laws of Islam, you could marry more than one wife without incurring any penalty.

The laws of nature are uniform and consistent through time. They will work in the same way under the same circumstances. Nothing has changed since Newton observed an apple falling to the ground in his garden; fruit still drops off trees in Trinity College, Cambridge. Once you notice that a piece of sodium dropped into water catches fire and rushes about on the surface of the water till it is consumed, you know that any piece of sodium will behave the same when dropped in water until the end of time. As a result we can discover beforehand what any material body will do under given circumstances and predict with complete confidence its behaviour pattern. I accept that people who know a lot more about science than I do may not be as cocksure as I am about the consistency of the laws of nature, but these laws are reliable enough for us to base our lives on them.

Hence, the first set of laws which will govern my construction work are natural in the sense they do not depend on my opinions or those of society in general. If I build a roof without adequate supporting beams, it will fall down. If I lay a foundation of concrete which has too much sand in it and too little cement, it will crumble because I have disobeyed certain chemical laws to do with bonding properties.

The second set of building laws does depend on human opinion and consent. It is not a natural law that if I build a bathroom extension which blocks out the light from the house next door it will collapse, yet it will come down all the same because the local authority has decreed that every dwelling is entitled to its own share of light and any structure which interferes with that right cannot stand.

Two conditions are necessary to make this second set of building regulations stick. The first is that public opinion is behind them. The Conservative Government's Poll Tax had to be repealed because public opinion was so vehemently opposed to it that many citizens refused to pay in spite of the penalties. The law prohibiting the sale of liquor in the United States was so widely flouted in the 1920s and 1930s that the Government eventually gave the whole thing up as a bad job. In the end, any law which has no public support is doomed.

The second condition is that building regulations should not conflict with natural laws. A local authority could decide that all the houses in its area should be built on the assumption that water flows upstream, all electric cables are made of rubber and fireplaces should be airtight. The council could even vote to abolish the law of gravity in its area, but that won't prevent a coping stone falling off the roof and braining the mayor. Building regulations which conflict with the laws of nature, no matter how enthusiastically they are endorsed by public opinion, will sooner or later prove to be unworkable.

Just as my DIY bathroom extension is governed by two sets of laws, so must any religion be that makes sense. There is a universal moral law which consists of certain statements of fact about human nature; someone has described natural law as a force working in history which tends to keep human beings human. We can find out what this law is by experience. It can neither be created nor rescinded by any human tribunal, however eminent, because it is a question not of opinion but of fact. The lessons of history show that when we behave in certain ways we act below our human capabilities and do violence to our own nature with terrible consequences. Take an ancient saying uttered long before the birth of modern science: 'He visits the sins of the fathers on the children unto the third and fourth generation of them that hate him, and shows mercy to thousands of them that love him and keep his commandments' (Exod. 20:5-6). It sounds the whim of a cruel or arbitrary deity when heard in isolation, but we know it to be neither a threat nor a warning but a cold statement of fact, borne out by the laws of heredity and environment. The lesson seems to be that if we defy the commandments of the natural law the race will eventually perish; co-operate with them and humanity will flourish. The Jews were saying 'This is the way the universe is made.' Centuries later, the German theologian Dietrich Bonhoeffer, reflecting from his prison cell on the evils of the Nazism which had put him there, wrote, 'The World is, in fact, so ordered that a basic respect for ultimate laws and human life is also the best means of self-preservation.'[6]

Material things are never tempted to contradict their own nature. It is the nature of matter to obey laws perfectly, with complete consistency and unerring precision. And that part of us which we share with the rest of creation has no option but to obey the laws appropriate to its nature. If we jump from a high building we have no more exemption from the law of gravity than a stone has. Material object and human being alike plunge to the ground. It is only that part of us which is different from the rest of nature which is free to disobey the natural law.

You can usually prove there is a moral law by imagining yourself in situations where you are in two minds between courses of action, one of which involves hazard. Do you go to the help of an old lady being mugged and risk being beaten up, or allow the instinct of self-preservation to take its course and pass by on the other side? You say you know what you ought to do. Why do you say that? It certainly isn't a prudent thing to do, it might even lead you to go against the life-force, that natural impulse which keeps us alive.

We also detect the presence of this moral law in our notion of progress, our conviction that certain forms of behaviour are better and truer than others, that it is not a matter of indifference whether people and societies behave according to the code of, say, Nazi rather than Christian morality. We don't shrug our shoulders when we come across examples of cruelty, torture and beastliness and say, 'Well, everyone to his own taste.' We staunchly insist that some moral ideas are to be preferred to others, and we can only do that because we are measuring them both against some standard, saying that one of them confirms to that standard more nearly than the other. Now, that's what I mean by moral law: a set of reasons capable of being understood by people generally for doing some things rather than others. Normal human beings have a sense they cannot get rid of, call it an instinct, about the sort of behaviour they ought to practise, whether they think of it as fair play, decency, conscience or obeying the moral law, and they feel in some strange way uncomfortable when they do wrong. That, I would submit, is a very widely shared experience.

It is true that people's understanding of what the moral law requires can vary to some extent from age to age and culture to culture, though the differences are not all that extreme. C. S.

Lewis compared the moral codes of ancient Egyptians, Babylonians, Hindus, Chinese, Greeks and Romans, and was struck by how very alike they were to each other and to the Judaeo-Christian version.[7] Underlying all the varieties of custom and law to be found in different societies and cultures, there are certain basic qualities which, however disguised, persist because any tolerable life is impossible without them – courage, justice, truthfulness and integrity, for example. We need courage to attempt anything new; without some semblance of justice, society would be in constant turmoil; truth is what keeps us in touch with reality; and it is integrity or constancy which guarantees our identity from day to day.

I make this moral law sound very absolute and fixed – as though the world were a kind of clockwork orange which has the inflexibility of some great, unbreakable machine, where cause and effect are precisely related. In fact, there is a wild unpredictable element in life: it can be a thing of poetry and fire, beauty and terror, horror and pity. So it may not always operate according to the laws of exact moral transactions, where good is rewarded by happiness and evil by misery. There is a strictly unpredictable dimension to human affairs which renders some tragedies inevitable and turns of grace possible.

Still, making full allowance for all that, the moral law is the safest guide to living. There is, however, another set of building regulations governing my DIY religion project that do depend on human convictions or opinions. They can be changed at will, though it is never done lightly. They are understandings about the nature of reality we have discovered in the company of those who see things as we do and share our views of the world. All religions have them, and they are hammered out sometimes after centuries of controversy, debate and argument. These statements of belief we call creeds.

Now, just as local building regulations must not conflict with natural law, so these beliefs that make up my religion must be grounded in statements of fact rather than my personal opinions. To call them a creed sounds rather formidable with its echoes of those sonorous and complex clauses which originated from ancient places like Nicaea after decades of theological argument. But a creed I must have if there is to be any consistency in my religious thought and behaviour. And it will need to be more than a collection of cheery platitudes – which would be the equivalent of those more eccentric local by-laws which express pious hopes rather than practical possibilities. I must try to root my beliefs in statements of fact.

All the great creeds claim to be statements of fact about the nature of the universe rather than idealistic fancies or arbitrary codes. For instance, when one of the Christian creeds asserts that 'except a man believe faithfully he *cannot* be saved', it is saying this is a fact; it's not what we fear might happen or hope to avoid; simply a flat assertion of the way the universe is. Take it or leave it. We can take such statements on trust or reject them as incredible, but to turn them into poetical truths or write them off as philosophical abstractions is to do violence to the purpose of creeds which are meant to provide a firm scaffolding of facts within which religion operates.

The theologian Nicholas Lash puts it this way. 'The confession that "God was in Christ, reconciling the world to himself" is to be construed as saying something, not only about God and man, but also about the way the world was, is and will be.'[8] That is an amazing claim – all the countless people, things and ideas we loosely call life are affected by that Pauline statement about the atonement.

Of course, if I'm starting my own religion I can put together any creed I choose. But doctrinal silliness does not long survive the cold light of reality. Sooner or later common sense will break in and expose any doctrinal silliness for what it is. An amazing truth may blast through and beyond my common sense, but if it outrages my common sense by being absurd, it will be exposed for what it is, utter nonsense rather than unutterable profundity.

When religious believers recite a creed they are not assenting to philosophical propositions but committing themselves to a view of the way things are, expressed in images and pictures which those wiser and holier than they have found helpful in stating facts that defy bald description. Religion is about a vision received by faith, but it is a vision of reality, and faith consists in a conviction of its reality. The Anglican theologian Austin Farrer wrote: 'The creed defines the contours of the world on which faith trains her eyes.'9 Without a creed, believers know neither how to call on God nor which God to call on.

This is why believers have been prepared both to endure and to inflict terrible things on behalf of their creeds. They are not engaged in logic-chopping, turning language games into homicidal pursuits. For them, their creeds embody their hold on reality, and to deviate by one hair's breadth from reality is like an astronaut returning to earth and missing his trajectory by a whisker. It may as well have been a million miles, nothing lies ahead of him but infinite space. A creed is like a key; it is a thing with a definite and precise shape which can only operate as a key at all if its distinctive notches and gaps remain absolutely fixed. Let one be worn down a fraction of an inch, and the key is useless. A hair's-breadth change and it has ceased to be a key at all. This is why early Christians battled for generations about the odd syllable of a Greek theological term in one of the creeds. The word in contention was tiny but the issue was for them a matter of life and death: it determined their view of the entire universe.

The building regulations of religion ought to be grounded in facts, but we have the right and duty to use our human freedom in responding to them, so I must modify what I said about the rigidity of creeds. Creeds summarise the beliefs of an abstraction – Identikit Man or Woman. They can't take account of the DIY element in all faith. Not even the wisest of religious founders has the power or right to prescribe exactly what form faith might take when the spirit of a religion possesses a unique human being. Creeds bear as much or as little resemblance to anyone's real-life faith as a railway timetable does to an actual journey. Bradshaw's railway guide sets out in a neat list of towns and times the standard journey from London to Manchester. But it's a paper pilgrimage. It takes no account of the possibility the train might be held up at Watford or be forced to make a detour around Wilmslow.

There can be no standard journey from unbelief to faith. If there were, the process would be so mechanical as to cast doubt on the reality of human freedom. People make rendezvous with their spiritual destiny by a route of their own choosing or by one thrust upon them by providence or circumstance. Certainly all wise pilgrims learn from the experience of those who have travelled that way before them. This is the value of formal statements of belief such as creeds. They set out the landmarks which most pilgrims have found essential in charting the route to a greatly desired destination. So if we are heading for the same place as others who have seen the world as we do and we find these reference points missing, we ought at least to worry whether we are likely to fetch up at the correct terminus.

Still, I can't just believe whatever takes my fancy. My religious structure is going to take a battering, not at the hands of the theologians, but in the teeth of the gales of life. And neither elegance nor ingenuity will hold it together: only the truth. And I use the word truth in the DIY sense, as when an architect or a surveyor declares a structure to be out of true, and so unlikely to stand up to rough handling or heavy weather. Toughness is one test that a building is true. Dorothy L. Sayers wrote: 'Pious worshippers do their gods little honour by treating them as something too sacred for rough handling; they only betray a fear lest the structure of religion should prove flimsy or false.'[10]

THE IMPORTANCE
OF OPTIMISM

The DIY enthusiast has got to be an optimist. Here he is, surrounded by a pile of bricks, endless planks of wood and various other materials, and already in his mind's eye he can see that elegant conservatory with marble fountain attracting whistles of admiration and secret sighs of envy from his neighbours. To make anything is an act of faith. It is a brave assumption that provided one measures accurately, saws straight and lays bricks according to a plumb-line, everything will come together obediently, serve its purpose, delight the eye and withstand harsh weather, boisterous children and nosy animals.

Can one trust the architect who drew the plans and the firm that supplied the materials? More fundamentally, can one trust oneself? It's a big undertaking for someone who has no practical turn of mind or natural dexterity. And he may be one of those people against whom the material world wages a constant war – he daren't let his car know that he's in a hurry to get somewhere, otherwise as a matter of principle it will refuse to start. So optimism is too weak a word to describe the verve with which he sets about defying those little demons that inhabit material things to do their worst.

The DIY religious enthusiast is disposed towards optimism because religion means looking around at the limit of one's senses and saying, 'There's got to be more than this, and that more is better.' And we have an ally in our life-impulse, which will assert itself against all odds in the concentration camp cell, in an open boat on a raging sea, in a hospital ward when the doctors have sadly shaken their heads, as well as in much less dramatic areas of our experience. We find it difficult to believe that there is a fundamental and permanent disharmony between our essential well-being and the facts of the world in which we live.

Some scholars say that the original impulse which makes us turn to religion is neither optimism nor pessimism but dread – fear of an unknown Something which has a mysterious drawing power that attracts us towards it. I wouldn't want to argue about that. But I am prepared to run the risk of academic scorn by insisting that a sense of awe, for that's what it is, by the very fact that it fascinates rather than repels us, puts us in a positive frame of mind. We wouldn't move towards the unknown unless we were expectant, eager for something exciting to happen to us. So, for me, religious dread is a sort of sub-category of optimism.

Those schools of philosophy which proclaim a fundamental pessimism about life have rarely become mass movements. The philosopher Bertrand Russell insisted that the only way to stay sane in a world doomed to nuclear extinction was to build one's life on a 'foundation of unshakeable despair'. But virtually everything Russell did was a denial of this gloomy philosophy. With glorious inconsistency, he radiated hope rather than despair and infused it into others when he spoke and suffered for a more humane society. Here was a man who at the age of ninety went to jail in a protest over nuclear weapons. When asked by reporters why as a very old man he was protesting about a possible catastrophe he would not live to witness, Russell replied, 'It is necessary to stand for things which will not come to pass until long after we are gone.'[11] If that is a philosophy built on a foundation of unshakeable despair then words have lost their meaning.

G. K. Chesterton wrote: 'No sceptics work sceptically; no fatalists work fatalistically; all without exception work on the principle that it is possible to assume what it is not possible to believe. No materialist who thinks his mind was made up for him by mud and blood and heredity has any hesitation in making up his mind.'[12]

It's worth asking how many world-weary pessimists who find life a burden and the whole creation unutterably wretched would, if offered it, refuse another life? Grant us youth, health, a sunny day and congenial company, and our whole philosophy of life changes or, rather, our system reverts to its default setting, that optimism pre-programmed in us by nature or destiny. For what is birth but the exchange of nothing for the possibility of everything? A zest for living wells up from within the profoundest depths of our being, and it is hard to believe that this raw energy was intended by nature to be suppressed or denied.

Human beings have consistently refused to put much faith in doctrines of pessimism which condemn the species to go against or smother the life-impulse. Paradoxically, even the martyr who seems to flout the life-impulse by embracing death does so on behalf of life, as a blazing declaration of its meaning and worth: he or she dies that someone may live.

Now we may reduce this species-optimism to a mere evolutionary urge. Psychologically, despair means the end of the life-impulse and therefore of evolution, which has relied for its propulsion on this sense in living creatures that they are equal to whatever challenges they face. The sceptic says this fundamental optimism of all living creatures is just a trick of nature to jolly them along and keep them moving on the long haul from the life-speck to the Nobel prize winner. Yet I find it hard to accept that the billion-year odyssey which has produced the sublimest achievements of the human spirit succeeded only because nature is a clever liar.

One might even argue that optimistic religion has been the essential precondition for enabling evolution to reach its highest stages. Instinct can be left to provide direction up to a certain point, but when our minds so develop that they can overrule our instincts, then whether humanity goes any further depends absolutely on the life-impulse becoming a conscious belief that reality smiles upon our struggle to achieve human maturity and well-being.

At this point I must insist that there are important differences between religious and natural optimism. Natural optimism is the brave belief that our best efforts must produce proportionately good results. They don't, as any reading of history will confirm. Of course, the converse *is* true, our worst efforts can and do make the world more of a living hell than it would otherwise be. But any gospel of inevitable progress finds shipwreck on the rocky reality of evil. It is not just our worst deeds but our very best intentions which can be taken, twisted and used destructively to frustrate our purposes and cause harm to us and to others. And natural optimism cannot come to terms with such harsh and inescapable realities.

All true, but I call a religion optimistic not because it is cheerful about the world's prospects but about those of the universe – it is confident that everything is properly under control. The universe makes sense in terms of its ultimate purpose, in spite of all the evil and suffering in it. It is possible to be at the same time a cosmic optimist and a worldly pessimist. We may be making a poor fist of that part of creation over which we have established control, but we have religious reasons for believing the universe itself is in good hands and that one day we shall get our act together and apply the larger law to the lesser realm. That is what I mean by religious optimism.

A DIY job confronts me with choices about materials and style and method. By plumping for optimistic religion I have made one choice which divides types of religion down the middle. I have decided to say Yes rather than No to life. There are only two great elemental philosophies, life-affirmation or life-denial, classically represented by Christianity and Buddhism. I don't want to get drawn into comparing great religions; I'm trying to start one of my own. But I permit myself one evocative image. Someone has pointed out that the Buddhist temple, the *stupa*, is shaped like a bubble, symbolising ephemerality, the fleeting nature of life, its final dissipation. By contrast, an apt symbol for Christianity is the egg – bursting with the possibilities of growth and perfection beyond its imagining – for how shall the egg know it will one day soar the skies as an eagle? Bubble or egg. The contrast in their message is stark: the only way to be happy is to be rid of existence, versus life is good and eternity still better.

Like most westerners I don't understand the subtleties of Buddhism, so it is both arrogant and foolish of me to write it off as a religious option when so many millions of Buddhists throughout the world draw strength from it to live heroic and virtuous lives. But its basic proposition is one that I would find insupportable. 'Birth is sorrowful, growth, decay, illness, death – all are sorrowful; separation from what we love, hating what cannot be avoided, craving for what cannot be attained, are sorrowful.'[13] I'm an Egg rather than a Bubble man. And from that choice another flows inevitably – and it is not a great philosophical issue, more a psychological one. In order to say Yes to life and so create an optimistic religion, I must decide which of two powerful inner forces will rule me and so determine whether mine will be a religion of fear or love.

These are the only two forces at work within me that can radically shape my life: love, the Yea-sayer and fear, the Nay-sayer.[14] Love is the principle of life within us and fear the death-bringer. To be fear-determined is to fight against life. It creates the sort of personality D. H. Lawrence once described as sunless, without radiance in itself and bidding to put the sun out in others. Jesus roundly declared that such folk have only one chance. Moral reform or positive thinking won't do the trick. They must start again from scratch; they must be born again: back into the egg and out again to new possibilities unhampered by fear.

Fear is an inner force which paralyses action. At its most effective, life always seeks to express itself spontaneously. Fear freezes the spontaneity of life; the more fearful we feel, the less alive we are. Fear achieves this by cutting us from all sources of life outside ourselves; it turns us in on ourselves, frightening us into building up defences against the fancied hostility of others. The psychologist would probably call these strategies defence-mechanisms. Defence-mechanisms against what? In the end, against life itself. And there is only one totally secure defence against life – death.

Of course there is a form of fear which is biologically necessary for our survival. It is our most dramatic teacher – we touch the naked flame once and we have learned the key lesson about fire for ever. It is our spur – we climb the vertical cliff because we fear the incoming tide; we risk losing our life in order to save it. But once fear ceases to be biologically necessary it becomes an inhibitor; indeed, spiritually demoralising, which is why much religion is concerned with its conquest. 'Fear not, only believe,' is the key demand of all true religion. Its aim is to convince those who believe that there is nothing to be afraid of.

But there is an important distinction here. To declare there is nothing to be afraid of cannot involve a promise to believers that none of the things they fear could possibly happen to them; that they are immune from unhappiness, suffering and death. That would be religion based on natural optimism – 'Don't worry, it will never happen – at least not to you' is its central text. And it's a religion which is of little value because we've lived long enough to know that many unpleasant things in life both can happen and have happened to us and unless we are very fortunate there's more of the same ahead.

There is, however, another possible meaning of the statement that there's nothing to be afraid of. It could mean that all the things we fear might well happen to us but, if and when they do, there's still nothing to be afraid of. True religion doesn't make promises it can't keep. It doesn't assure us that this thing rather than that one will happen to us because we believe; instead, it says that regardless of what happens to us, it will be all right in the end. The ugliest facts we can possibly confront will not vanish if we close our eyes, they're real all right, but they are not to be feared.

No religion which offers us an escape from reality can withstand the invasion of a brutal truth. It cannot offer us protection from life, defence against the consequences of our folly or ignorance, escape from the iron laws of our existence. Real religion will save us from fear but not from the things we are rightly afraid of. When President Franklin D. Roosevelt told the American people in the depths of the economic depression of 1933, 'The only thing we have to fear is fear itself', he was making a profoundly religious statement from a political platform. Jesus put it differently: 'Be of good cheer, I have overcome the world' (John 16:33).

Religions which purport to offer security against fearsome reality have been hugely destructive forces in human history, for real religion can never be a means to an ulterior end – to hide us from an uncomfortable truth, bolster an unjust society, embalm dead traditions or hold at bay the perils of maturity. When people have a secret hidden fear at the centre of their consciousness, they will clutch at anything they think might save them, especially power-religions based on money, the state, the proletariat, the Führer, or God the Heavenly Dictator. But in the end to bow the knee to such concepts is to worship gods that are our moral inferiors. Religion means to worship the more-than-human; to play around with forces that are less-than-human is magic.

What, then, does it mean for a religion to be love-determined? If fear constricts, locks us in, cuts us off from people, then love must be an imaginative reaching out to others in order to acknowledge their absolute right to a claim on our time and attention. Love pushes back the boundaries of our existence, for it is the drive to unite all that is separate in time, space and condition. And it is obvious that in our life-time there are many forms of separation we cannot overcome. We must meet our death as unfinished creatures. And the possibility is offered that love's work of making us whole has begun and must continue until it is complete.

One great bonus of optimism is that it glories in the fun of life. This is also one of the advantages of DIY. Many people who take up DIY do it as a form of recreation. What they produce may be both ornamental or useful to them, but the real reward for the enormous effort they invest in their project is the amount of pleasure they get out of it. The job may be painstaking and long drawn out but it's not a burden; in fact, it's a joy. What about DIY religion, then? Are we allowed to have fun whilst putting our religion together, or is religion one of those subjects too serious to be treated lightly?

I don't believe that *any* subject is too serious to be funny about, though there are occasions when humour would be an inappropriate way of dealing with it. After all, fun actually depends on solemnity for its point; we can make jokes only about serious things; frivolous things already are a joke. I would go further and say that unremitting seriousness is essentially irreligious. I mentioned idolatry earlier. To take anything with undue solemnity in an imperfect world is to make an idol of it. An outstanding feature of two of the most godless regimes of the twentieth century, Nazism and Communism, was their humourlessness. Neither Hitler nor Stalin was noted for his wit. To lack a sense of humour is to be less than fully human. Hazlitt in an essay on humour, writes, 'Man is the only animal that weeps and laughs; for he is the only animal who is struck with the difference between what things are and what they ought to be.' And much religion is taken up with that difference.

We find it hard to give ourselves permission to laugh about religious matters. We have this deeply ingrained sense that we should always be serious about serious things and unutterably solemn about the most serious thing of all, God. Yet the words 'funny' and 'serious' are not opposites. The opposite of 'funny' is 'unfunny'; the opposite of 'serious' is 'frivolous'. So religion will always be a serious subject and sometimes a very funny one as well.

Religion has always had this funny side. Cathedrals were built in the great ages of faith, yet they are filled with gargoyles – grotesquely funny stone figures staring down from walls and roof so that when worshippers lifted their eyes towards heaven, they might be struck both by the sense of God's majesty and the absurdity of the human condition. Or, in some of the medieval morality plays, the spectators engage in silly clowning at the foot of the cross, and in the York cycle the Roman soldiers preparing the cross for the crucifixion bore holes in the wrong places – as a result, Jesus's hands cannot be nailed to its cross-beam.

Religious festivals such as the medieval Feast of Fools were occasions when believers felt able to make fun of all the things, people and rites they took with the utmost seriousness throughout the rest of the year. The monks appointed one of their number Lord of Misrule to preside over a mock eucharist. He chanted a Litany of Folly during which an ass was worshipped and the communicants brayed their responses. It seems that when people were secure in their religion they could afford to be jokey about it. On the other hand, in a secular age swept by doubt, many believers feel threatened when someone pokes fun at their religion.

It's back to the word 'religion' again – that which binds everything together, the totality of life united in whatever or whoever we call our God: life and death, time and eternity, spirit and matter, the things which call out tears and those which evoke laughter. You can no more leave out humour from a religious account of the world than exclude the continent of Asia from an inventory of its land masses. We need a comic perspective on religion to preserve us from making idiots of ourselves by according our self-made idols undue respect.

True religion has the power to make us joyful about the most serious things. It is significant that the great epic poem in which

Dante offers a comprehensive account of life in the form of an allegory of the human soul's progress towards God is called *The Divine Comedy*. Though religion is a serious business it need not be utterly solemn. We are allowed to have fun. We may undertake our DIY project with optimistic zest and find raw material for our religion in the lighter side of life.

AN APTITUDE FOR MAKING THINGS

All kinds of human skills are needed for DIY. They might range from manual dexterity, through practical judgement, a good eye for design and the measurement of length or distance to sheer dogged persistence and physical strength. When the particular piece of DIY has to do with making a religion, what human aptitudes are needed for the process? Is it the thinking, feeling or acting part of us which is most engaged?

We know that people can believe passionately in false gods or in gods that incite them to do terrible things. This suggests that our religious faculty is firmly rooted in our emotions, which don't make moral judgements about things and take no account of truth or error; they are simply *there*. Could we then say that our feelings are the essential tool of religion; whatever triggers them is our god, at least for the time being? The French philosopher Pascal said that when God wants to make a point with his children, he plants it deeper than the mind, in the instinct.

Certainly, any religion which didn't engage our feelings would be a very cold and arid thing and should probably be more accurately described as a philosophy or even a set of opinions. A great religious thinker, Frederich Schleiermacher, wrote, 'Religion is a sense and taste for the Infinite.' He said that our conscious life has three parts: knowing, feeling and willing. The first gives rise to science and the third to morality, but the second, feeling, is where religion takes hold. We experience awe or dependence or fear or some other deep emotion and only afterwards do we ponder what has happened and come up with religious ideas, dogmas and creeds to describe it. We often value things because they appeal to our feelings; indeed, the novelist George Eliot went so far as to claim that our beliefs are just different names for our emotions.

Yet common sense suggests that our feelings alone aren't enough to sustain our religion or any other aspect of our lives. Is there such a thing as pure feeling? As someone has said, pure feeling is pure bunk. If you say to me 'She was deeply moved', almost as a reflex I ask 'By what?' We must have a feeling *about* something or someone – a beloved person, a cherished possession, or even a set of ideas which add up to an invented god called Moo.

Our feelings would be little more than the fever of over-active glands unless directed towards some object. The psychologist might say that feelings are subjective responses to external stimuli – I laugh at a certain comedian's jokes but you find them distasteful; abstract art excites you but leaves me baffled. Our feelings change because of alterations in our ideas, sensations and perceptions. We confess that we disliked someone at first sight but when we got to know him we became very fond of him. Knowledge transformed our feelings.

Certainly, religion has traditionally been considered primarily a disposition of the heart – that's what the poets and mystics and sages have said. But our beliefs would be completely at the mercy of our moods unless our intelligence stood guard over our heart and allowed entrance only to whatever it considered to be true. Something must be seen as having the right to direct our feelings otherwise we would bob around like corks on the tide, carried along on waves of sentimentality, which is emotion without responsibility, the loosest possible attachment to reality.

We must have some way of discriminating between religious feelings. Did the same emotion possess the ancient Greek dancing in honour of the wine-god Dionysus, the whirling dervish running the gauntlet of his comrades' swords, the Muslim charging into battle in a Holy War, the Buddhist attempting to extinguish all desire and the early Christian martyr going to the stake? It is hard to isolate such emotions from the beliefs with which they are associated, for each assumes a different theory of what life's goal is and how it may be achieved.

Most Protestants observing a Roman Mass cannot feel what a Roman Catholic communicant feels because they do not believe that the bread and wine literally become the body and blood of Christ. They may show the reverence fitting in any place of worship and at a solemn ceremony – and more, a certain shared loyalty to a common Lord – but their state of mind must be different. And whether Roman Catholics or Protestants are right about the meaning of the Eucharist cannot be measured by the intensity of emotion they show. No subjective emotion can be a ground for believing in an objective truth about the universe.

So far as we know, only thinking beings have any instinct for religion at all. Animals obviously *feel* things but nobody, however besotted with the creatures, has ever offered evidence that they have religious tendencies. Scientists have uncovered cave-paintings of animal-gods done by early Man but nowhere has there been found even the crudest animal-scrawl depicting anything, let alone a creaturely deity. There is proof that human beings in the Nile delta once bowed the knee to crocodile gods but nothing to suggest that crocodiles returned the compliment. Like art, religion is the signature of the human being.

Even if we tried, we couldn't shut out our mind from sharing in all the religious experiences we undergo. And in order to talk about religion, which is one element in its 'religiousness' – the impulse, as the apostle Paul put it, 'to give a reason for the faith that is in us' – we must use mental and verbal constructions. Reason's role in our religious faculty seems to be to find arguments for our convictions.

We might describe the link between mind and emotion in our religious life by saying that belief is an emotion triggered by an idea. In Nigel Dennis's play, the Moo Idea was different from the Ega Idea, which in turn would be different from the Christian Idea, and each of these ideas might stimulate in different people or in the same person at different times the emotion we call belief. There may be psychological or cultural or other reasons why we settle for one religious idea rather than another, but that idea has got to be true *for us*, it must feel right in our gut before it can become a conviction. We cannot argue someone into a religious belief if his or her feelings are set against it.

There is another school of thought which insists that our religious faculty is located neither in the mind nor the emotions but in the will. What matters is not what we believe but what we do – in the preacher's epigram, religion is not a way of talking but a way of walking. A Victorian poet put it like this:

> Let prideful priests do battle about creeds,
> The Church is mine that does the most Christlike deeds.

Religion's function is not to make us think or give us a warm tingle of emotion but to enable us to act in ways that offer a fuller life. So long as whatever it is people look upon as their God *works*, they needn't be particularly bothered about its identity or even whether it exists at all. Those who think this way say the goal of religion is not belief in an abstract deity but in more abundant, satisfying life. If a religion is able to offer *that*, then the intellectual questions can safely be shelved. According to this view, religion is not a theory of anything; it is the art of life seeking ever higher and better techniques. So call your God Moo or Jehovah or Allah or whatever you like, if he does the trick that's all that matters.

This notion of religion as a pattern of behaviour is certainly one of the great themes of the Old Testament. 'What does the Lord require of you, but that you should do justly, love mercy and walk humbly with your God?' asks the prophet Micah (Mic. 6:8). The supreme expression of religion according to both Jews and Muslims is the law, torah and sharī'ah. And Plato taught that the true service of God is moral obedience. God's existence and nature are demonstrated not by philosophical arguments but by following his commandments. As Jesus put it, 'Why do you call me "Lord, Lord," but don't do the things I command you?' (Luke 6:46).

The link between our thinking and our conduct is by no means one-way; we don't just ponder a course of action and then do it. It can work the other way round. We can act in such a way as to change our thinking. For instance, if we behave towards a stranger as though he were a valued friend we invariably end up thinking well of him. So some would say that living as though God exists conjures him into being, and he needs no other form of existence. Whether he is *there* in an objective sense, above the bright blue sky or brooding on chaos before the universe began, is a matter which might baffle our minds for ever, but the way we behave reveals the nature of our ultimate loyalties and so sketches out the dimensions of the God we truly believe in. One very practical way of being religious is to live *as if* God exists and see what happens.

In sum, then, our religious faculty is driven by our mind, emotions and will, in proportions which differ not just *for* each of us but *within* each of us from day to day. But they are all involved. Religion is a way of life which unites the intellectual and emotional sides of our nature. Take worship as a distinctive religious activity. You can't worship something you don't recognise – hence, knowledge; nor is worship possible without feelings of fear, yearning or gratitude – hence, emotion; and worship involves us in doing things – perhaps praying, sacrificing, singing – hence, willing. Religion which doesn't involve our minds degenerates into magic; without feeling, it's an intellectual game, and, unless it changes something in the real world, it is an irrelevance.

The priority we give to the different elements in our religious faculty will be reflected in our style of religious obedience. We may walk the mystical path to God, or the ethical or the liturgical or the path of social action. Whole schools of theology or even religious denominations have been founded on the varying pressures of mind, heart and will in the human religious faculty.

Perhaps it's a little misleading to distinguish so sharply between our minds and emotions and will. Religion is the response of our whole personality to the whole of life. Through it we grasp what the world is about. We can't pretend to know the tinest fraction of all that can be known about the world, but we are still prepared to take the risk of thinking and saying things which sum it up. Our religion compresses all the contents of the world or, rather, puts a frame round them. It may be a mental trick, but it is one deeply ingrained in us that we want the multiplicity of separate objects to be absorbed in one single underlying reality. So we talk about 'life' when we don't just mean biological vitality but simply everything – people, things, history, culture, ideas and the rest. And we use the word 'existence' not just to mean an irreducible minimum, bare survival, but the supreme maximum – all there is in contrast to nothingness. When we crow, 'The world's our oyster!' we aren't talking about global conquest but psychological expectation.

There is another aptitude which is much to be prized in making things. The accomplished DIY enthusiast can see in his mind's eye the finished product even though those not gifted with his skills gaze around on a scene of chaos, a jumble of raw material and general untidiness. He can project his imagination beyond the parts to the whole. This is the gift of inspiration. In an often-quoted dictum, the American inventor Thomas Edison defined genius as one per cent inspiration and ninety-nine per cent perspiration. This applies not just to works of genius but most human endeavours. This magic one per cent makes the difference between a crude mechanical operation and a creative act. And the term 'inspiration' belongs as much in the realm of religion as of art. It has the double meaning of being stimulated to great heights of creativity or of being permeated by some spirit.

It is not essential that the DIY enthusiast should be inspired. One could tackle DIY as a series of problems to which solutions are offered in handbook or diagrams. We are shown where one piece fits into another, which tools are apt for a particular task and how to assemble awkward or complicated bits of machinery. This is a form of construction widely used not only in DIY but on the mass production line or factory floor – the reduction of the process of making things to a number of problems which can be resolved simply and speedily.

It would not be hard to think up a DIY religion which operates on just that principle, offering ready-made solutions to the problems thrown up by life. After all, that is why some people turn to religion: they are up against it and assume that God, in one form or another, will help them. When people who never normally give God a thought offer fervent prayers in times of crisis, they aren't usually looking to change their philosophy of life; they want a God-inspired solution to a particular problem.

Take the problem-solving mentality at work in the religion I know best, Christianity. 'Christ is the answer!' bellows the evangelist when it's as plain as a pikestaff that far from being the answer, Christ is often the problem. What are we to make of some of his harsher demands, that we should hate our parents or pluck an eye out or sell up and give the proceeds to the poor? He was an enigma to his own time, and the mystery has not been banished by twenty centuries of scholarly reflection on his life and words. Who would claim to have access to the mind of Jesus on a thousand and one issues of our time? Would he approve of western civilisation or the dedication of costly and magnificent churches to him? Would the way we educate our children or treat the aged or spend our leisure time, deal with prisoners or organise our industry please him? Could we know how he might regard the EEC, nuclear energy, television, population control and on and on?

Perhaps Christianity became a problem-solving religion when, instead of it converting Europe as is widely supposed, European culture converted Christianity from being a near-eastern apocalyptic faith into a western problem-solving ideology to be harnessed to the needs of an optimistic and thrusting scientific civilisation. The early Christians abandoned all hope for a doomed world and turned their attention to a better one. By contrast, over the centuries, western Christianity has increasingly pledged its authority to the fevered dreams of secular optimists.

Religion as a problem-solving device usually disappoints those who turn to it for guidance. Some problems are strictly insoluble – death, for instance. There is no way the Grim Reaper can be banished from human life, though we may be able to stave off his arrival by medical or technological virtuosity. Some religions offer a satisfying life for their devotees on the other side of the dark curtain: they transfer the whole set of values connected with death into another realm, that of eternity, or offer another chance on this earth through the process of reincarnation. But no religion has a solution to the problem of death. Or of evil, for that matter. The higher religions show how death and evil can be transcended as experiences but not solved as problems in the sense that they no longer exist.

We don't have to tackle DIY as an obstacle course of problems and solutions. It could be a creative enterprise where we operate by the canons of art rather than the rules of industrial production; free expression instead of mechanical assembly. We can act by inspiration. The point about any work of art, however modest, is that we find there more than the artist put in. Walt Whitman said that music is what awakens in you when you are reminded by the instruments. And in the presence of Turner's or Tintoretto's pictures John Ruskin felt as a man might feel in the presence of a supernatural being. True artists seem to penetrate life's secret depths and there find some thing or being or force which exists independently of them.

Confronted by a truly creative work, we say that it's a revelation to us. What does that mean? Dorothy L. Sayers has well described the creative process in writing – which, incidentally, is one of the purest forms of DIY.[15] She shows how a work of art generates a life of its own, over and above the effort put into its creation. Firstly, there is the book as thought, an Idea in the writer's mind; secondly, there is the book as written, the Energy, the sheer sweat and blood that goes into its writing; thirdly, there is the book as read, the Power of its effect on the responsive mind.

For example, suppose we take a trip to the theatre to watch a new play. We like the idea, that's why we queued for tickets in the first place. 'A most intriguing subject,' we say. And during the play we are conscious of the energy the writer has put into his or her work, but we are not quite sure where it all leads. 'How is it going to work out?' we wonder. Then, when the final curtain falls, we may feel quite differently about the play. We can think of it as a whole and see how its various parts came together to produce something inside our mind which is *more* than the sum total of the emotions we felt whilst watching it. It has been a revelation to us, increasingly charged with power as it went through the various stages of the DIY process. And if we react positively to the play, its power will be communicated to us; we enter into its spirit, and our lives are enriched as a consequence.

There are obvious limitations to the human creative process. Besides the finite extent of our talents there is the innate resistance of the material with which we are working. There are things we can do with words and things we cannot do with them. If we are concerned with drama, we come up against the fact that actors are only human, they have their weaknesses. A sculptor has to wrestle with the properties of stone or bronze because there are limits to its plasticity or strength or texture.

All creativity is restricted by the basic material it uses. I fancy this is why Judaism, Christianity and Islam insist that God created the world out of nothing – there was no raw material to resist his will, so all he created was good. Equally, all things must be held in existence by him because if they were created from nothing there was no original state to which they could revert. My DIY table will continue to exist if I leave the room because the material of which it is made has a rigidity that holds it together. Even without me, the woodness of wood enables it to go on. But if the world was created out of nothing, then presumably were God to withdraw from it, since its existence depends on the material he used, everything would fall apart. That's why Paul said to the Athenians, 'In him we live and move and have our being' (Acts 17:28).

When we have given all we can to religion as a human enterprise – the effort and skill, the wisdom and sacrifice – we reach the point where we can do no more. We must have faith that if our religion is well wrought, we shall find there more than we put into it. Like a good play's power to create in us something that wasn't there before, we hope ultimate reality will reveal something of itself to us, not just as truth – this is the way the world really is – but as power – this is what you can do.

If, then, my DIY work is truly inspired, it will be invested with a power that was not in the original material nor in the skill and dedication I bring to shaping it. Shaping what? What is the raw material of religion?

8 RAW MATERIAL

The subject matter of religion is anything and everything. All that is being thought, experienced, said and done by anybody could be its raw material. We can look out through innumerable windows upon an astonishing landscape. What G. K. Chesterton wrote about Christianity applies to any serious religion:

You cannot evade the issue of God; whether you talk about pigs or the binomial theory you are still talking about him. If Christianity should happen to be true – that is to say, if its God is the real God of the universe – then defending it may mean talking about anything and everything. Things can be irrelevant to the proposition that Christianity is false, but nothing can be irrelevant to the proposition that Christianity is true. Zulus, gardening, butchers' shops, lunatic asylums, housemaids and the French revolution – all these things not only may have something to do with God, but must have something to do with him if he really lives and reigns.[16]

People who say religion is an illusion don't usually deny the facts religion deals with; they just claim that religious people misinterpret these facts by reading into them things which aren't there. For instance, according to John's gospel, when Jesus cried out, 'Father, glorify thy name,' a voice from heaven answered him. But John goes on to say, 'The crowd standing by heard it and said that it had thundered. Others said, "An angel has spoken to him"' (John 12:28,29). It was the same fact, a strange unearthly response to Jesus's cry, but those present interpreted it in different ways: as a voice from heaven or thunder or an angel.

We may interpret the facts of our experience as the raw material of religion in different ways according to our preconceptions. Those who believe religion is about fear concentrate on terrifying facts such as earthquakes or snake gods or the occult. Those who talk of God as a Father-projection will see the core of religion in the facts of parent–child relationships. Or those who identify God with Fate will read all kinds of significant things into the conformation of the stars or the throw of dice or patterns in tea leaves. Christians treat as supremely important a number of facts to do with the history and experience of a near-eastern Semitic people called the Jews. From all the facts of experience human beings select those which confirm and sustain the master-idea underlying their religion.

Religion is not the only activity which takes all the facts of existence as its raw material. So does science. A glossary of science would stretch from A for Anthropology to Z for Zoology and in the process encompass much of life. Art too can roam throughout all our experience in search of subject matter. Religion, science and art all cover the whole world of the possible. But they don't put equal significance on the same bits of it. For instance, the law of gravity may fascinate a physicist but will be of marginal interest to a theologian unless he's looking for a sermon illustration. An artist may be entranced by his wife's face whereas the pure mathematician might regard his own spouse as a rather elaborate differential equation, though if he has any sense he'll keep the opinion to himself.

Whether we look at the world through the eyes of the scientist, the artist or the religious person, we have to decide how we will judge what we see. We put the facts in some kind of order in terms of the amount of attention we want to pay them. In other words, we attach some valuation to them. And we could define religious faith as the willingness and capacity to give Something or Someone supreme valuation.

Religion, then, is about arranging everything which makes up our lives in some kind of order of priority, putting what we call our God at the top of the list. Now, there are two common ways of valuing things; one is typical of the scientist, the other of the artist. We may value something for what we can do with it – its usefulness, or for what it is – its inherent interest. The civil engineer, for instance, may get sensuous pleasure in running wet cement through his fingers but he is more likely to value it for its properties as a bridge-building material than for its porridge-like consistency. On the other hand, an artist may have no interest in the sort of structure you could build with several rows of bricks but she still exhibits them in a gallery as contemporary art because she is entranced by their beauty.

These two types of valuation may overlap. Take architecture, for instance. The architect as scientist is concerned to create a strong, sound, efficient building whilst the artist in her wishes it to be a beautifully proportioned structure which decorates the sky-line. But there's no point in erecting an aesthetically pleasing building if it comes crashing to the ground in the first roaring gale. For her, the test of usefulness is the dominant one. An artist may expect her custom-built car to be mechanically sound and reliable but it is chiefly for its sleek lines and perfect proportions that she has chosen it.

Whilst the scientist and artist are busy assigning different values to the facts of experience, what are religious people doing? Which of the two forms of valuation do they put on the contents of their world? Are they chiefly concerned with usefulness or beauty? The answer is both. From time immemorial, the object of religion has been both precious in its own right – therefore shrouded in taboos and sacred rites – and also the source of strength and support, an aid for living. Thus the God who in one part of the Bible is to be worshipped 'in spirit and in truth' (John 4:24), is in another part referred to as 'a very present help in trouble' (Ps 46:1). Religions such as Judaism, Christianity and Islam apply this twofold valu-ation to human life. They say that individuals have unique value as the creation or even children of God – intrinsic worth – but their highest destiny is to be servants of God – usefulness.

It is obvious why neither science's test of valuation as usefulness alone nor art's valuation as intrinsic worth alone would do for religion, which is primarily concerned with people rather than things. To judge other people solely by their usefulness to us would reduce them to chattels or slaves, means to our end. So that won't do. But to use the intrinsic worth test alone must result in a sort of mutual admiration society. We can't spend our lives gazing adoringly at one another – not unless we are poets of the mystical school. But when the two forms of valuation are combined, you arrive at the position where people gladly serve their fellows because they have the highest possible estimate of the intrinsic worth of the human personality regardless of its qualities or achievements.

The object of our religion, then, is that which we treasure above all else in life. To put it in more traditional religious language, it is what we worship, either through formal rites and ceremonies or by privately acknowledging its significance. And this valuation is not as cold-blooded or deliberate as I have made it sound. It may be that we don't ponder and then choose judiciously as though we were selecting a library book. The self-evident (to us) truth of our choice may hit us and the penny drops. On the other hand, things may only fall into place almost imperceptibly. We discover what we value above all by painful process of trial and error, of false starts and new beginnings. It's that seed growing secretly Jesus talked about.

But however it happens, by dramatic discovery or inch-by-inch realisation, there enters into our valuation the element of absoluteness or inevitability. Science says some things are; morality says some things are better than others; religion says that one thing is supremely valuable and we would be better off if we believed in it. So when in popular speech we talk about 'making a religion' of something, we mean we've put it in a category of its own. It will take more than ordinary persuasion to get us to change our view of it.

There are a number of conditions this supremely valuable something must meet if it is to be taken seriously and it is our common sense, rather than any theological knowledge, which lays down what they are. First, whatever we regard as supremely valuable must express itself in a response of our whole personality to the whole of life. If it is something which simply engages our partial interest or has relevance solely to our emotional life or intellectual pursuits or social activities, then it is not valuable enough: it cannot command our total loyalty because there are things to which it does not apply. 'I live for cricket,' says a friend of mine. Cricket may indeed be his great love to the point where he is besotted by the game, but if he also looks to it for the kind of explanations religion has always claimed to offer about the whole meaning of life, it is hard to see how cricket meets the bill. It doesn't cease to be a game because fanatics choose to turn it into a life-long obsession. There is much more to life than sportsmanship, though no doubt things would be much pleasanter if we were all prepared to play the game in our dealings with others.

Nor can this supreme something be a totally private preoccupation like a great painting we keep hidden in a bank vault and only bring out occasionally to gloat over. If this value is confined to our most private existence and ceases to have any significance the moment we encounter another person or step outside our front door, then it may meet the intrinsic worth test but not that of usefulness: it has no bearing on our relationships. And that puts a real question mark against its true worth because we cannot contract out of the human race – none of us is born in complete isolation and few of us go on to live and die separated from human contact.

This point about human contact suggests that there is an important difference in the way religion, as opposed to science and art, values the contents of the world. The scientist can peer through his microscope as the objective observer of the tiny cosmos in a drop of water but the micro-organisms aren't glaring back at him, sizing him up whilst he is studying them. At least, so far as we know they aren't. Equally, the artist may look at Venice from a very personal perspective but the Bridge of Sighs isn't simultaneously making up its mind whether the artist is any good as a painter. But when we human beings look at the world we cannot avoid being part of it. It's not just that we value it; it also values us – I am part of your world and you are part of mine. The religious question isn't just: 'What do we make of the world?' but also 'What does the world make of us?' As Jesus said, 'With what judgement you judge, you will be judged' (Matt. 7:2).

Deciding what is supremely valuable in our lives may be a purely personal, subjective thing, but at some point we have to put this judgement to the test of practical relevance in the business of everyday living unless it is to remain a set of ideas we toy with or a mere emotional indulgence.

And whatever we attach supreme value to in our lives will not just be the best thing amongst many more, but will offer us a principle of valuation, a bench-mark for testing the worth of any-thing else – its value is the source and standard of all our other values. Put differently, our general view of existence is seen through the lens of whatever we hold supremely valuable in our lives.

Since we all have something to which we tend to give priority amidst whatever else clamours for our attention, we are to that extent religious, even if our bank statement or a photograph of our family or a mirror offers the most accurate representation of our deity. George Cantwell Smith has written, 'The only true atheist is he who loves no one and whom no one loves; who does not care for truth, sees no beauty, strives for no justice; who knows no courage or joy, finds no meaning and has lost all hope.'[17] There are few people, even members of the League of Militant Godless, who meet those qualifications.

What, then, do I supremely value? It can't be money because I may lose it, or sex because such appetites wane, or ambition because as the years take their toll once desirable goals recede beyond my reach. I suppose if I were pushed, I would confess, a little coyly: it is when I try to do what is right and stand for the truth as best I can, that the conviction is borne in on me that I'm hitting a sort of bedrock in my life, in some way aligning myself with its ultimate reality. This, I believe, is the way things are meant to be; qualities such as love, goodness, truth and beauty seem not to be inventions but revelations; they are not what I import into my life but what I find there. These are what I value supremely.

I feel that such love, goodness, beauty and truth as I have known have been 'givens' of my existence in the sense that Euclid's geo-metric propositions are 'given' – we can't get back beyond them and examine the suppositions on which they rest. We 'see' that they are what they are. Love, truth, beauty and goodness seem to exist in their own right. They aren't easily confused with each other nor can any of them be subordinated to the others. They are not subject to the law of nature which decrees that a gain here must mean a loss somewhere else. They are capable of infinite increment. The amount of each available to us can increase without limit, yet even then, they can only be expressed imperfectly here on earth, and so hint at some realm where they are fully realised. They convince us that the universe has high mysteries which will stretch us to our limits and beyond. Unlike Alexander the Great we need never weep because we have no more worlds to conquer.

I believe it is through the presence of love, goodness, truth and beauty in my life that I am in touch with ultimate reality, and I sense this isn't just a personal fancy on my part, but the rational order of things. The practical proof of all this is that there is nothing worthwhile I have achieved in which love, truth, beauty and goodness played no part. And when I analyse my moral failures, it is not hard to locate the cause in my unwillingness or incapacity to stand by the loving, the true, the beautiful or the good at some point.

All this I see, but there is a paradox here. On the one hand, I don't believe that absolute values of love, truth, beauty and goodness depend for their existence on my acceptance of them, or anyone else's for that matter. On the other hand, I don't know of any realm or order of existence where these qualities are to be found in pure form as abstractions, floating in the air as it were – any more than there could be a memory which nobody remembers or a joke that nobody has made. How can one talk of meaning unless there is a meaner? I cannot visualise or imagine goodness as an abstract value, but when I encounter a good person, I get the point. I don't really know what beauty is as an intangible quality, but once I've seen a few examples, I have some bench-mark. And I have seen people torture their bodies and minds to destruction in pursuit of truth – *their* truth, which means more to them than life itself. Like love, beauty, goodness and truth become real for me when they are chosen as supremely valuable by human beings whose natures as a consequence have become loving, beautiful, good and true.

Since every evidence of moral values known to me is to be found in personality, this also suggests that the reality in which they are grounded is personal. Hence I must stop talking about God as It. He (or She) would be more appropriate. And God has no right to demand these moral qualities from me unless he also possesses them, otherwise I would be his moral superior. But God does demand them from me through my dutiful sense that I am *required* or *meant* to do certain things and not do others. I believe, therefore, that he is the source of the moral qualities I demonstrate at my best.

At this point I run up against the objection that I'm really confusing religion and morality; that religion is just ethics in its Sunday suit. In fact, the relationship between religion and morality has been very complex throughout history; never one of simple identification. In the early dawn of our life as a species, religion had little connection with morality. We followed tribal or clan custom rather than any individual impulses, good or bad. Morality was just the law of the tribe because religion was a social thing; it was the group as a whole which was related to the god or gods. To do the right thing was the same thing as keeping the deity happy; to do wrong was to stir up his wrath by breaking the law of the tribe. Early religion was little more than a technique for attaining certain practical benefits such as making crops grow, curing diseases, punishing enemies and winning battles. Such religion didn't necessarily encourage morality as we understand the term. Some gods were the moral inferiors of those who worshipped them, demanding actions such as child-sacrifice from which the average human being might have recoiled in horror but for the belief that the god required them.

Far from being identical with religion, morality in the ancient world was often a high-principled reaction against it. Poets, reformers and philosophers in Greece and Rome protested in the name of morality against the practices of temple, altar and cult. Only when tribal and national religion widened to become universal and narrowed to individual obedience was it possible to talk of religion and morality as separate spheres of human existence, though still related. After all, what is the point in worshipping a god who is our moral inferior?

All the great religions are rooted in the conviction that when

71

believers live by such values as goodness, truth and beauty, love, honour and purity, they are striking the rock-bottom of reality; they've hit upon the key to the meaning and purpose of life and their proper place in it.

To revert to my DIY analogy. I am not the first enthusiast in the history of DIY who has attempted to make a chair or re-tile my bathroom. When finished, the chair may be my very own and one of countless varieties, but it must bear some relationship to every other chair in the world otherwise it couldn't sustain my weight in a sitting position. Equally, though I'd like to think my DIY religion is my very own creation, both in style and content it must be similar to other attempts to base religion on moral values. For it is the ultimate insanity to have moral values which are exclusive to me and bear no relation to those of others. One can no more have private moral values than a private sun and moon.

And there are widely shared moral convictions that overleap cultural, racial and geographical boundaries. We do not excuse treachery, tyranny, brutality, cruelty and lying, on the grounds that foreigners in their own land or different ethnic groups or classes from ours have their own funny ways of doing things, and good luck to them – though we have to take care that we don't condemn what we don't understand and confuse strangeness with vice when we observe the actions of people whose culture is alien to ours. Rhetoric about the universal conscience of humanity may sound high-flown and even priggish but it means something.

All this depends on one huge assumption: that there is a real distinction between good and evil, that love is better than hate, truth than lies and honour than treachery; that in any human endeavour, the better is to be preferred to the worse. Whoever will not concede this much is not just rejecting my argument but losing touch with reality as well. The acid test is simple: we must try living as though distinctions between good and evil are of no account, that hate rather than love should govern all our relation-ships, that lying is a more effective strategy than truth-telling and that to betray one's country, friends or principles pays long-term dividends in happiness and personal security. We shall probably conclude madness and chaos lie that way.

So, if I am to start from rock-bottom assembling my DIY

eligion, my point of departure is not in anything dramatic or eerie
o do with strange rituals or sacred ceremonies, but in finding new
lepth and significance in boring and unexciting things like doing
ny duty and standing by old-fashioned virtues such as loyalty, love
nd honour, regardless of the cost.

9 EXPERTS

It gives the DIY enthusiast great satisfaction to make something unaided. Nevertheless, when confronted by a particularly tough challenge, it is reassuring to know there is a vast amount of experience around on which we can draw. There is no conceivable problem we can face that someone else in the DIY business hasn't had to overcome.

When the business happens to be religion, the rather daunting name we give to such experts is saints – a term which conjures up visions of pale aesthetes gliding three feet off the ground, exuding clouds of superheated piety, a lily in one hand and a copy of Foxe's *Martyrs* in the other. In fact, saints have been an amazing variety of human types, though with certain things in common regardless of the religious labels they wear. Saints are practical proof that a religion works. They claim to speak about ultimate reality from observation and experience rather than from theory or speculation.

As we have seen, moral values don't mean much to us as abstractions floating in the upper air; we only get a clear sight of them when they are incarnate in people. The religious faculty of saints has been developed to such an unusual degree that their relationship with supernatural reality as the ground of their moral values is transparently clear. They are consumed by a sense, in Baron Von Hugel's phrase, of the Isness of God which lights up the whole of their lives and works itself out in severity towards themselves and tenderness towards others.

Just as DIY enthusiasts have widely differing aptitudes and ranges of skills, so the moral and spiritual development of human beings varies greatly, with the vast majority of us rarely doing anything particularly heroic about our faith. Then along come the trail-blazers, the saints who give meaning and precision to our rather vague religious sentiments by showing us what has been there all the time, but invisible to us until that moment. In every field, our knowledge of the universe grows sluggishly until some genius makes a giant leap of understanding. The fundamental truths of mathematics have been self-evident since time began but it took a special kind of mind to perceive them and teach the rest of us.

Once a fresh idea of God has been disclosed, thousands can then get the point and acknowledge it. The new type of character which this religion creates can be imitated, though only a tiny number will be able to achieve the apparently effortless virtuosity of the true expert, who turns into an art what to the rest of us is a plodding struggle. I once saw a TV documentary about Picasso, and at one point the artist picked up a pencil and in a single stroke drew a perfect circle on a blank sheet of paper. It seemed simple, but a life-time of hard practice went into that single sweeping movement. If religion is the art of living seeking ever higher techniques, the saint turns spiritual discipline into a form of grace.

It is true of science and art and music, and of religion and morality, that the many are able to see with the eyes of the few. General knowledge of God comes to us, like any other knowledge, by one person standing on another's shoulders to see further. As the apostle Paul acknowledged, he was a debtor to Greeks and Jews, Gentiles and Barbarians – Socrates and Plato as well as Moses and Isaiah were amongst his teachers. All the great trail-blazers are natural educators, they have the power of revealing to others at least something of what they think, feel and have seen.

Whereas the theologian with due humility offers an opinion, the saint announces starkly, 'I know!' He or she presents solid evidence of religious truth. Evelyn Underhill puts it like this: 'As the fish could not have come into existence without water and the bird guarantees the supporting though invisible air, so the undying fact of sanctity guarantees God.'[18] We would know much less of the reality of God without the witness of the saints, and it is hard to account for their extraordinary power and achievements in any other way than by their confidence in and reliance upon this reality.

When saints are around, things happen in the world. Religion ceases to be a matter of argument and theory and speculation, of contending theologians and bickering ecclesiastical politicians. There has been change, and most noticeably in the character of the saints themselves. There occurs a re-direction of life so dramatic that Paul could talk in terms of a 'new creature'. It could be argued that only those in whom this costly and genuine change has begun have any real idea what religion is about. For saints, religion means the release of love and creative energy that comes from sharing, however imperfectly, the life of God, and it produces radical change, both in personal character and in the life of society.

Just a slender wire can carry a powerful electric current and a small window let in a lot of sunlight, so ordinary people can stand for extraordinary ideas. That is how Christianity came into the world, by ordinary people being seized by an extraordinary idea which demanded, 'Stand by me, fight for me and if necessary die for me!' The saint is often an ordinary person, a two-talent religious figure who has been invaded, possessed by an extraordinary force, and transformed into a living example of what religion can do.

Of course, many of the best-known saints could not have been described as run-of-the-mill characters even before their life-changing encounters with God. St Francis, Wesley, St Teresa were powerful personalities anyway and were capable of demonstrating outstanding religious gifts even without that quality we call sanctity. But when sanctity and religious genius are combined in one personality, humanity's understanding of religious reality leaps forward and something new and exciting stirs in human affairs.

The saints don't usually claim to have discovered something, they say they have received everything. They insist that all they know and feel about religion is a free gift from outside themselves rather than a prize won by painstaking struggle. The words of St John would summarise the feelings of Christian saints, 'We love him, because he first loved us' (1 John 4:19) Ultimate reality as they have experienced it bursts into their lives with an overplus of meaning which they strain language to get across to others. For them, God as ultimate reality is a paradoxical combination of the completely Unknowable and the intimately Known – which underlines the 'givenness' of the experience, for how could the human mind work out for itself such awesome concepts?

Once this gift has been received, everything changes for saints. It is a transforming energy which drives them to attempt hard things and conform to new standards. The Bible and Church history are crammed with examples. Moses at the burning bush, Isaiah in the temple, Paul on the Damascus road, Augustine told to abandon a promising academic career, St Francis ordered to repair God's house, Luther in the monastery at Erfurt poring over Romans, Wesley at Aldersgate Street, and so on and on. New lives and careers open up, priorities radically change, especially about worldly things. What saints *are* becomes much more important than what they *have*; the lust for things wanes, for only those with no entrenched interests can follow an ideal single-mindedly. In some cases poverty is enthusiastically embraced as a bride, in others there is a new-found carelessness about material things. Either way, absolute surrender to an ultimate power changes every perspective on the world.

Perhaps the most distinctive activity of the saint is the one which seems to have least to do with practical necessity or the natural needs of the human creature – prayer. The evolution of prayer from terror-ridden begging to the ecstatic adoration of the saint is a remarkable chapter in human history. Like art and poetry, music and philosophy, prayer is an expansion of the human consciousness in directions whose tiniest beginnings cannot be detected in any other creature. The stimulus seems to come from beyond the world.

It is a matter of common sense that religion demands prayer. To assert that reality is personal, that God is like a loving Father or a great King and do nothing to make contact with him is to render the claim meaningless or irrelevant. Ultimate reality may as well be a blind force rather than a personality if it does not invite and return communication. If personal being does not mean having an urge towards self-disclosure and welcoming it in return, it means nothing.

According to one authority on these matters, prayer is putting oneself in the presence of God. Saints live there. There is none of that wrenching change of gear which normal believers experience when they are called upon to pray – a godly discipline whose end is to be welcomed with a certain amount of shame-faced relief. 'That's done for the day, then,' we say with quiet satisfaction as though we had disposed of the washing-up and cleared up the kitchen. For the saint, the Isness of God makes set praying a formality. It is a little like the Isness of breathing. We do it all the time and only when the doctor says to us, 'Breathe deeply', do we become conscious of it. For the saint, the process may never become conscious: God is not so much a Power to be approached in a prayerful attitude as an all-encompassing environment to abide in.

This does not mean that all saints have been paragons of conventional virtue. The records show that some were quirky, irascible, difficult to live or work with, and often without understanding of the human frailties of ordinary believers. Sometimes their imperfections were plain for anyone to see, but whilst dispassionate observers might doubt many things about them, one thing was beyond argument: their utter conviction that when they prayed a real Someone answered them and when they listened a real Someone addressed them. They are guarantors of God's existence.

Our astonishment at the passionate extremity of the saint's character is mingled with relief that we cannot realistically share it. If they were a different species, those saints who also have religious genius would be described as exotics. They demonstrate human nature at its most extravagant and are therefore always in danger of committing, in William James's words, error by excess. Their devoutness can shade into fanaticism, their purity become priggishness and their self-severity might lead them to leave undiscovered some of the hidden riches of their personalities. But those who must live and deal with saints, and are therefore on the receiving end of such errors of excess, would say the price is worth paying in order to have such undeniable proof that a religion works.

In the end, however, it's not that saints perform the strict religious duties ordinary folk neglect: they do things which wouldn't occur to the rest of us. In the face of a crying evil or an almighty mess in human affairs, their reactions are often totally unexpected. They home in unerringly on the creative possibility in the most unpromising situation. They operate not as lawyers – 'These are the rules!' – but as artists – 'Let's see what we can make of this.' Inventiveness is the key to their faith; they are never without an initiative in the face of the gloomiest circumstances – an unexpected word, an inspired but costly gesture.

In a word, they are gracious. Grace is that unexpected element we can neither command nor deserve which enters a situation from outside and seeks saving possibilities within it. In this sense, saints are agents of hope. They expect everything from their God but nothing from others, and therefore they are neither surprised nor disappointed when their initiatives are rejected and they attract hatred or indifference. Their strategies are dictated neither by prudence nor the demands of strict justice. For them nothing is at stake, whether pride or life itself. Louis Pasteur, who discovered techniques of vaccination against several diseases, said that fortune favours the prepared mind; the saint insists that the future favours the gracious spirit. They are the leaven of history, rarely transforming it by dramatic upheaval but by countless imperceptible but significant demonstrations of the grace of God in action.

These, then, are the experts on whose knowledge I can draw if I get out of my depth in this DIY exercise. Most of the great religions throw up saints who show marked similarities in their reactions to the Transcendent which are more fundamental than differences in language or outlook or official religious allegiance. Their experiences do not cancel one another out, the Muslim Sufi does not nullify the Christian hermit's truth, the Buddhist monk cannot deny the Hindu fakir's witness, holiness in the Sikh saint does not contradict the moral sublimity of the Taoist shaman. On the contrary, saints reinforce and confirm each other's experience, even when their teaching would be at odds. Saints seem to confirm the existence of religion pure and simple. They believe in the vivid actualness of ultimate reality and are drawn by the same Spirit into such knowledge of it as they can achieve.

There is appreciation of the saintly character right across the spectrum of religions. Christians venerated the Jew Martin Buber; Buddhists made pilgrimage to sit at the feet of the Hindu swami Sri Aurobindo; Gandhi's soul-mate was an Anglican missionary C. F. Andrewes, whilst Martin Luther King saw Gandhi as his great guiding light; the Hindu Rabindranath Tagore's wisdom was treasured by Christian scholars and Muslim Arabs revered the White Father Charles Foucauld. And Mother Teresa moves with universal acceptance amongst the people of many faiths. The turning circle of sanctity whirls on. Holy wisdom knows no confessional boundaries.

Now let's be clear: I am not arguing that the differences between great religions are of no importance because the saintly character seems to transcend them. But it's a fair question. If there is such spiritual and moral kinship between the saints of many religions, what is the point of all the inter-religious rivalry? No doubt sordid issues to do with land and territory and influence have much to do with it. But it is also a fact of both history and geography that the main cultures of the world have been sufficiently different to constitute different ways of being human. There are Chinese, Indian, African, Semitic and European ways of being human, and each one offers a distinctive way of being religious, though of course religious faith can overleap cultural barriers. There are American Buddhists and Arab Christians, African Jews and Chinese Muslims. But other things being equal, where you are born will most likely decide what your religion is, should you have one at all.

All humanity is to be found in every religion, its stark blacks and whites and the endless shades of grey in between. For every evidence of evil to be found within another tradition, the honest believer must own up to a parallel within his own. The social oppression of the Hindu caste system is matched by a South African apartheid maintained by Scriptural warrant; the ferocity of the Muslim incursions into Europe in the fourteenth century must be weighed alongside the Crusaders' rampage through the Near East. Hindus incinerated widows on their husbands' funeral pyres, Christians burned witches; Shia and Sunni Muslims tear Arab countries apart, Protestant and Catholic communities in

Northern Ireland live in bloody turmoil. Christians oppress Jews, Jews oppress Palestinians. What are we to make of this messy, morally ambiguous stuff we call religion?

How are we to judge between religions apparently equally capable of producing saintly personalities of towering moral and spiritual insight? Do we need to? Well, reverting to my DIY analogy, I could say of a chair: 'Mine is the truly standard chair; yours may look like one but when it is put to the test it will fail, so you had better start making chairs my way.' Or I could say: 'Your chair is not my chair, but it is an expression of your way of doing things; I still think mine is better, but each to his own chair.' Or I might even say: 'Neither of us has got it right yet. Let's share our skills and experience and keep on trying.'

There are religious believers in all great faiths who insist they and they alone have a hold on truth and others must learn to walk their way or be damned. They insist their truth exactly expresses ultimate reality; anyone else's claim to truth must therefore be illusory. They might have a case if divine truth could be contained in the form of propositions. But what if the Supreme Reality is simply Unknowable, beyond the reach of all human thought? If so, then all religious metaphors are inexact, images vague and blurred, language faltering. It is foolhardy to claim we have a monopoly of the truth when we have to use finite minds to comprehend it and human words and images to express it.

It is, of course, possible to insist that we have a greater share of the truth in religion without insisting we also have a monopoly of salvation. I might think my chair is better than yours, but I don't doubt you can sit on yours comfortably. We are entitled to think that believers in other religions are mistaken in some of their beliefs, and they no doubt return the compliment, but we gladly concede that no religion able to produce saintly character is without saving power. Even within our own tradition there are undoubted saints, some of whose religious beliefs seemed wrong-headed or even juvenile, but who has the right to consign them to the outer darkness?

There are two other possibilities. One is that each of the great religions may be right for the people of a particular culture and time; it has been an effective means of grounding them in ultimate reality. It is equally possible that none of humanity's religions has yet got it right. They are all to some degree imperfect, prone to error and short-sightedness, but on a journey whose compass-bearing will be modified as they encounter other travellers who started from a different point and can back their estimates of the terrain ahead by hard-won experience.

Who knows? These vast questions of comparative religion are so complex and inconclusive they make our heads ache. And that very fact can easily offer us an excuse for hiding in the fog. The general is always easier to cope with than the particular. We find it less painful to pray for the whole vast world and its apparently insoluble problems than for half a dozen people right under our noses where the point of contact between the prayer and the reality to which it refers cannot be avoided. The world in the round cannot make costly demands on us; our neighbour does. It is not the general principle but the particular case that challenges us most.

William Blake wrote: 'He who would do good to another must do it in Minute Particulars.' That is the genius of the saint – he or she thinks it supremely important to do good in minute particulars. The vague generalities of faith represent telescopic religion – the distant, blurred view in which the fine detail merges with the background. The saint's chosen instrument is the microscope, through which, as Jesus might say, the foreground is occupied by the individual hairs of our head, the single sparrow that falls to the ground or the tiny coin lost by a housewife.

General debate about religion is fascinating and totally absorbing; it is the religion of the specific instance that is costly. Ask any saint. Wrote A. E. Whitham, 'We shall recover the joy of our religion when we stop generalising, turn away from the big maps and trace God in the little diary of our obscure life. The reality is in the practical instance, and there is no joy, no full-blooded, deeply grounded religious experience unless we find God in particular decisions.'[19]

Finding God in individual decisions. In DIY language that means: stop worrying about the ground-plan of the New Jerusalem and get on with sawing a specific piece of wood for that particular chair.

10 PEOPLE DOING THINGS TOGETHER

I can see I need help with this DIY project. I might manage with difficulty to assemble a simple bookcase but to build, say, a house would require a range of skills I don't have. And it's not just the advice and example of the ten-talent experts I need. I also require people just like me, two-talent amateur builders, to help not only with the fetching and carrying but also to cheer me up when it looks as though we'll never get the slates on or keep the wind out.

Now what common sense thinks a good idea, my growing understanding of religion makes essential. I've located my God, the one to whom I give supreme valuation in my life, in a personal reality which I relate to when I live by moral values such as love, truth, goodness and beauty. But I can't stand for such splendid things in isolation. As I pointed out earlier, it is no more possible to have private moral values than to own a private sun and moon. They've got to be worked out in my dealings with other people, because the self I express them through only exists in personal relationships. I am human, and that's what humanity is, people linked to one another.

My personality exists in and by communication.[20] I am the creation of a personal relationship. I begin life by being helplessly dependent on my parents, I end it in the hands of whoever cares for me, pronounces me dead and lays me to rest, and in between I rely on other people in a thousand ways. If I am not cared for from birth

I perish. The giving and receiving of affection is a condition of my survival. My growth is a growth in communication and so in community. I am a social being even when I am cut off from other people in solitude or enforced isolation. Even the mind of the hermit or the person in solitary confinement is peopled by thoughts which were once shared, that he has brought with him into seclusion, the fruit of common experience and tradition.

It is this simple fact which makes the notion of a one-person religion impossible. *Religere* refers to that which binds everything together: the very structure of human experience, dependent as it is on mutual relationships, is religious in texture. Duty is one way of relating to others, affection is another, and through both, love, truth, goodness and beauty keep me in touch with ultimate reality by controlling my relationships with others. As moral values they are maimed and diminished when I try to express them in isolation.

The religious life, then, is one that is dominated by this belief in the centrality of personal relationships. The religious word is fellowship, communion both with others and with the Other, for once we begin to reflect on our mutual interdependence, the idea of God arises naturally. Our reason's gift is an urge to universalise our experience, and if our personal relationships are central to that experience, then the universal which begins to take shape is that of universal personality.

For much of the time we take for granted the network of relationships which determines our personal life, but every now and then it pushes its way to the forefront of our consciousness; we become aware of our mutuality. Then we have the need to mark, celebrate and strengthen it. We do something special together to express the truth that all our life consists of doing things together. We may dance together or sing or share a common meal or perform other ceremonies which bond us, such as reciting our common beliefs or telling stories about our past. These are corporate, symbolic acts pointing beyond themselves to the core of our religious life as grounded in our togetherness. And when we do these things we feel that combination of fascination and awe which signifies the presence of the Holy Other. In that place, at that time, together, we thrust down into ultimate reality, taking the shoes off our feet because we are on holy ground, the vicinity of the sacred.

Using the image Martin Buber made famous, for much of our lives I am an I to someone else's Thou, but when I meet with others on these sacred occasions, we are all fused into a corporate I. And where is the Thou to whom we can relate as a communal personality? It can only be God, and he must be an infinite person because he is one part of a relationship, but capable of relating to all communities at all times, and therefore eternal.

Because this network of relationships through which we do things together is all-encompassing, and so many tendrils of our lives interweave with those of others, this is a club of which I cannot be a corresponding member. In the field of religion we cannot act through agents, whether priests, gurus, theologians or even charismatic leaders. In many areas of life a division of labour can operate between the one who does the thinking and the one who acts. In building my house, for example, I may employ an architect who thinks the project out to the last detail and then hands over to a builder who does the actual work. But I cannot enter into fellowship through agents, allowing someone else to make links and establish relationships on my behalf. I cannot endorse a creed, sign up on the dotted line and then leave the rest to the professionals. Because religion can only be real as something people do together, I must be fully present to the experience and bear its costs and pleasures.

All the religious ceremonials in which a community engages have their roots in the real-life relationships of those people. Religious ceremonial for its own sake is either fantasy or magic. There are enough key events in community life to provide material for ceremonial observance – birth, marriage and death, seed-time and harvest, war, tragedy, and disaster, landmarks in national life and history. All these can be symbolised and brought within the celebration of the common life. Ceremonies and rites are never self-justifying. They mark events which are important to the religious community because they are central to the life of the community generally. And the symbols at the heart of these ceremonies are very ordinary, making connections not with some special world but with everyday existence – bread, wine, water and a bowl and towel.

By far the most important thing religious people do together is pray. Prayer is the decisive way a community indicates its confidence that God exists, that it is not engaged in some psychological or social wild-goose chase. By the fact that a group of people – of every type and condition, the brilliant and the simple, the powerful and the weak, the old and the young – are prepared to address God and believe themselves to be addressed by him is as near a guarantee as one can get that God is present, hears and understands.

But talking with God is obviously a special kind of communication. It would be foolish to claim that no one has ever been addressed by God in the tones of human speech – there are many strange stories in the annals of religion about sensible sane people claiming that God spoke to them as a human being speaks to a friend – yet because God is utterly distinct from everything and every other being in creation, his speech style must usually be quite unlike any other form of communication.

Because we cannot expect God to speak in what we understand by human speech, we are in strange territory where we need to draw on the wisdom and holiness of a community which has for centuries become attuned to God's unique language. They have vast experience in communicating with God and in interpreting his special way of communicating with them. The apostle John advised one of the early Christian communities to 'test the spirits whether they be of God' (1 John 4:1). All kinds of strange things happen when people fall under the influence of religion. They can stray across the narrow dividing line which separates rapture from hysteria; they may exhibit the symptoms of over-excitement and imagine things or confuse the unknowable with the nonsensical.

Jesus's words, 'By their fruits you shall know them' (Matt.7:16), are as good a test as any of whether believers have been in real communication with God. We may assume that God has no interest in gossip; he doesn't talk for the sake of it. When he communicates, it is to get results, therefore so-called God-thoughts which leave no impress on the character of the Christian community are highly suspect. It may not always be possible to decide whether believers have grown in inner holiness as a result of conversation with God, but it's usually apparent whether their honesty and truthfulness have been affected.

It is through its prayers that the religious community, besides confirming God's existence, also sketches out his nature and attributes. It is not unknown for God to be addressed as a Heavenly Policeman, or a Divine Father Christmas, an All-Powerful Tyrant or a sentimental Old Pal as well as the more orthodox endorsements of his character. Therefore, in the act of addressing God, the community reveals its own true nature, its deepest desires and darkest fears, its honest understanding of what its purposes are.

What the community believes from the bottom of its heart is expressed not through dogmas or creeds but in its prayers. There is a kind of skeleton creed shared by the great religions such as Christianity, Judaism and Islam which is sketched out in their common prayer-life. No one has put the essence of this basic religion more succinctly than G. K. Chesterton. He wrote, 'The world does not explain itself, yet it does have meaning and therefore a Meaner. It is beautiful but not perfect; hence, the reality of evil and the need for rescue. Assuming the world were created by a good deity, his creatures would wish to thank him; sure enough, there is an in-built human desire to worship. And conscience points to God's existence because there must be someone to whom we owe duty.'[21] The community of faith is invited to address God in such prayerful truths. In fact, there is little reality in a religious idea which cannot be cast in the form of prayer.

In all true prayer, what is spoken could only be said to God, which is why it jars when someone prays in his own words yet it's clear that, though he's formally addressing God, he is really preaching a sermon at his fellow-worshippers. That is not prayer but exhibitionism. We can't mistake talk addressed to God either for talking to other human beings or even talking to ourselves. It's not just that the words are different, they would be crashingly inappropriate or even bizarre if they expressed our dealings with other human beings.

Through its prayer-life, the community takes for granted the presence of God. At the beginning of every service there isn't a sort of philosophical recitation of the classical proofs for the existence of God, nor is there any mumbo-jumbo to find out whether God is waiting to hear from his people in the way a medium might ask her spirit-control to rap three times on the table if contact has been established. The great religions make no provision for the possibility that God is not present at all times and in every place.

There are many stories in the history of religion about God communicating with people through visions or unearthly voices or other inexplicable happenings. Some of these events have had consequences so amazing they cannot be dismissed out of hand as hysteria or wish-fulfilment. Paul's vision of Christ on the Damascus road changed the whole destiny of Christianity. But what happened to him would make no sense except against the background of two communities called Christianity and Judaism and the conflict between them. Paul's change of heart and mind would by any standard be a baffling phenomenon, but the knowledge and experience of the people of God was needed to spell out its religious significance.

Believers seek to know the will of God, but if God doesn't speak to them as one person converses with another, how can they know what God wants them to do? Leaving aside exotic practices such as bibliomancy where a person opens a Bible at random, stabs a verse of Scripture and then takes what it says as God's word to him or her, it is the community of faith which is the most reliable guide to what God wants one of its members to do – as, for instance, when someone believes he or she is being called by God to be a minister or a missionary. That personal conviction may be so intense that no other opinion, even that of a Church, can shake it. Yet the religious community must still put such personal understandings of God's will to the test, for what is a unique event in an individual's life has occurred many times before in the experience of the community as a whole.

These people doing religious things together are imperfect human beings without any guarantee they won't make mistakes. They can be wrong, even when giving advice in the most solemn matters. Thus, until recently, a woman who felt called to the ordained ministry of the Anglican Church would meet with a regretful but firm judgement that her sense of call was mistaken; she had misread God's will for her. The body of believers called Anglicans are now having different thoughts. God's will for them is being painfully and prayerfully argued out and new truth seems to be emerging. The whole process has been so protracted and agonising precisely because God doesn't speak to those who believe in him like an invisible person telling others what he wants in plain human language.

Much prayer to God is taken up with asking him for things. And very often we don't get them. 'O God, get me off this shop-lifting charge,' I might pray. If I actually committed the offence and God did intervene to destroy the evidence or strike dead the only witness who saw me slip the tin of salmon in my pocket, then we would be in the realms of magic. So when I pray that some catastrophe may not come my way, I'm not trying to shape reality to my selfish ends, I'm saying to God, 'Help me to live through this.' I mustn't regard it as a count against God's existence that he doesn't modify the operation of the laws of the universe to make me happy. As Jesus warned us, God sends the rain on the just and the unjust. The good and bad alike seem both to suffer or to flourish according to no discernible moral pattern. D.Z. Phillips puts it this way, 'Praying to a God for whom all things are possible is to love God whatever is the case.[22]

There is a technique in broadcasting called white noise. White noise is necessary in radio because there are no pictures; the only way the listener knows his set is switched on and working normally is through the sounds that come out of the speaker. But there are times, in drama for example, when the script calls for pregnant pauses, utter silence. At such times, the listener doesn't know whether the programme has gone off the air or not – there is nothing to be heard. So the engineers fill the silence with white noise. It is a special sound track which is subtly different from dead silence; not so much a hiss, more the faintest suggestion of presence, as though someone were there but saying nothing.

The religious community comes to regard God's silence as a form of white noise. It is the silence not of absence but of communication. There was a time when I would have thought the phrase 'silent communication' was a contradiction in terms until my computer went on the blink and I lost all my punctuation marks – full stops, semi-colons, capitals, everything. All I had was endless chunks of text, great streams of words, and I suddenly realised how important silence is in communication. For that's what punctuation marks are. They are symbols of silence where you pause, hesitate, ponder, take a breath.

All great artists are masters at speaking through silence – the object left out of the picture just where you'd expect it to be; the void in architecture; the caesura, that pause in the middle of a line of verse; the note withheld in music. Recall, for instance, those five thundering Hallelujahs at the climax of the Hallelujah Chorus – four of them, and then a pause that seems to last for ever, and then the crashing fifth. And in the throbbing silence is an unspoken Hallelujah as piercing as the others.

But how does the community know that it is sharing the silence of communication? It must be a possibility that heaven is silent because it is empty. Well, in everyday life we know the difference between dead and living silences. We go into a restaurant and see two couples at adjacent tables and both are silent, but there is all the difference in the world between the two forms of silence. In one case the silence is a void, and in the other it is filled with presence. In one case they are silent because they have nothing left to say, and in the other they are silent because they have passed beyond the need for words.

All these people praying together might have got it wrong: Heaven could be silent because it is empty. But whereas the individual believer could well be the victim of subjectivism, when hundreds of millions of people who believe in one God insist that prayer works, then that's as near as possible to objective evidence in such matters.

Something strange has happened to my DIY project. It began as something I do myself, but once I start doing it with others, it changes its nature. I abandon the responsibility for carrying the whole thing myself and, in return, I become part of a much more elaborate operation. It's what happens when a solo instrumentalist begins to play as part of an orchestra. He no longer has the freedom to deliver the melody in any way and at any pace he chooses, to improvise at will and add to or subtract from the original score. Heard in isolation, any individual instrumentalist's contribution may not make much sense, but when blended with that of the rest of the orchestra, the result has a range and complexity beyond the reach of a single player.

11

IT'S A MYSTERY

TO ME

My DIY project is no longer mine. Once people start doing religious things together, they lose their right to individual ownership of what they are doing, though they get the compensation of greater probability they are on the right track. It's also a matter of common sense that whereas an individual can easily be deluded, if a great number of people approach whatever or whoever they think of as God and don't get any response, they will abandon that form of religion and look elsewhere. And if no human beings anywhere throughout history had been answered when they cried to their gods, then religion itself would have vanished from the face of the earth as a discredited stage in human development.

Once religion becomes something we do together, then those ceremonies which express our togetherness, because they are concerned to root us ever more deeply in ultimate reality, generate a strange power which takes us out of our usual pattern of existence. Though we have the original power of decision in choosing what we value most in life, once that choice is made, there takes place a strange transformation. What we have chosen does not remain our possession but takes possession of us.

This ultimate reality which our fellowship celebrates inspires in us a strange combination of wariness and fascination. We've felt it in other areas of our lives at those times when nerving ourselves to do perilous things – to climb Everest or jump by parachute or sail single-handedly round the world. At such times we were both really scared and truly excited – we know what the poet meant when he wrote, 'I felt myself so small, so great.' The challenge was daunting but we met it with exhilaration. We would describe as sacred those moments when we were stretched beyond our limits and survived.

Sacred – that's the word we use to describe the 'specialness' of the reality which we have discovered to be of incomparable worth to us. It cannot be compared to anything else in our lives; the moment we weigh it in the balance against other things, however precious, it has lost that uniqueness which makes it sacred. And as we encounter it, we recognise we are out of our depth. We cannot grasp its full nature because our minds have come up against a kind of frontier on the other side of which tantalising realities are glimpsed like dim shapes in the mist. It is truly a mighty mystery.

That word 'mystery' needs a little explanation. When we hear it in common speech we usually think of an Agatha Christie or Ruth Rendell murder story. Mystery is often confused with or used interchangeably for two other terms – 'problem' and 'puzzle'. The Mystery of the Loch Ness Monster; the M4 Murder Mystery; Government Poll Tax Replacement Mystery. The first might be a puzzle, the second a problem, the third not so much a mystery, more a muddle. A puzzle is a faulty way of looking at something and can be solved by altering our perspective. The fact that ships did not fall off the edge of the earth was a puzzle to those who believed the earth was flat. The puzzle was solved when people stopped thinking like flat-earthers. And a problem exists because sufficient information is lacking or not being properly applied. The correct use of information will solve the problem.

The sacred is not a puzzle; whichever way we look at it we find it beyond our comprehension. Nor is it a problem. If additional information finally explains it then it wasn't sacred in the first place. The sacred is mysterious because its essence cannot be grasped by our minds; it can only be described and explored, and always inadequately. Any proposed explanation of a mystery casts only limited light on unquenchable darkness. So when we describe the sacred as mysterious, we mean it is a counterpoint between knowledge and mystery. If there were nothing unknown about it, it would cease to be sacred and become an everyday fact. If it were totally mysterious it could hardly hold our interest for very long since what is totally unknown may as well not exist.

Any religion worth having must be able to explain enough to make sense of the world but mustn't make the mistake of trying to explain everything, otherwise we shall end up with a pedantic little faith. All true religion observes a proper reticence about the mysterious element in life – not that which is as yet unknown until the Big Brains unravel it but what will remain for ever unknowable. 'Mystery' – the Greek term means to close one's mouth. Every attempt to capture its essence in words is doomed to failure.

Demosthenes wrote, 'If you cannot bear the candle, how will you face the sun?' And we cannot bear the candle. We live within the finest of tolerances. If our temperatures rise or fall by a mere handful of degrees we die. Too much air pressure on us or too little and we implode or explode. Too much noise, too much silence and we go mad. We can only bear a tiny fraction of the totality of reality. The rest is mystery. Yet there is something about the unknown that lures us on. Thousands of people go to Loch Ness every summer hoping to catch a glimpse of the monster. In medieval times, scholars scoured the earth looking for the philosopher's stone that would turn base metal into gold. There is magnetism in mystery, which is why religion has never vanished from the human race. And part of its attraction is the exciting possibility that what is strictly beyond understanding may help us to understand everything else. I suppose the sun is a rough and ready example. It is the one thing we cannot look at and yet by its light we can look at everything else. It is both a blaze and a blur, sharply outlining everything whilst itself remaining as fluid as fire.

Through its urge to gaze into the sun, religion has exercised a kind of fascination for the human mind since time immemorial. Great religious thinkers have ransacked language to find images that would convey this sense of mystery surrounding whatever they had discovered to be of supreme worth. Plato wrote of flickering shadows on the wall of a cave; Paul of baffling reflections in a mirror. These images have a common characteristic – they tantalise with the promise that maybe there's a chink of light in the darkness. Perhaps the hem of the curtain may be raised just a fraction to allow us to glimpse the reality beyond.

So the sacred is hedged about with mystery, but we must be circumspect. If whatever we celebrate as having supreme valuation assumes the character of the sacred, we had better choose with care. We have taken it for granted that the sacred is morally admirable, a force for good. But that obviously depends on what it is we elevate to ultimate value in our lives. The sacred can be a destructive rather than a creative force. We may cry 'Lord, Lord' and mean something degrading or unreal by it. People, as we know, are capable of doing terrible things in the name of religion.

For this reason, I want to abandon the word sacred and substitute for it another word which is totally unambiguous: holy. It too means that which is set apart from everything else but it has no murky history; there is no touch of evil or even earthiness attached to it. It is not, I grant you, a jolly word. There is a crystalline, almost forbidding purity about it; all the frigidity of starlight. But it is a word which throughout history has been peculiarly associated with ultimate reality as personal.

Traditionally, holiness is a special quality of God. It isn't like any other of the divine attributes such as goodness or righteousness or mercy. It is what makes God godly. We could imagine a God who is not good or righteous or loving, but we could not conceive of a God who is not holy. So holiness conveys the sense of the supernatural, of transcendent power.

Let's take a practical example of the way human understanding of the holiness associated with ultimate reality developed amongst a people who have a genius for religion, the Jews. By way of illustration, I use the Old Testament not as a sacred book but as a slab of history with the roof off. There was nothing rarefied about holiness as the Jews in the Bible encountered it. It struck them not as a cold abstraction but as white-hot energy. In the early morning of their human understanding of God, his holiness seemed to have no ethical content – it was raw energy – and to get in its way was fatal, as a poor chap called Uzzah discovered. He tried to be helpful and touched the holy of holies, the ark of the covenant, in order to steady it as it travelled over rough ground. He was struck dead for his pains. Or there were two sons of Aaron, Nadab and Abihu, both priests, who decided to jazz up the liturgy and put burning coals in their censers in a way that was not customary, and were burnt to a crisp as a result.

Divine holiness as it was understood in the earlier part of the Old Testament often vented itself in sheer fury. The Hebrew words which describe the inner fire of God's being mean snorting, foaming, boiling under pressure. When the OT writers sought suitable metaphors for the holy God they described him as a roaring lion, a hissing serpent, a ravening beast, an angry bear – untamed natural power. We can understand why the American poet Walt Whitman wrote that in all true religion there is a touch of animal heat.

We may laugh at the credulity of these ancients who seriously believed that God could react with homicidal fury when his holiness was impugned. Yet the lesson that the Jews draw from Uzzah, Nadab and Abihu is that when people lose their wary sense that there is a boundary between the holy and the everyday, when they no longer feel the urge to take the shoes off their feet as they stepped on to holy ground, then moral disintegration and often disaster follow.

In the progress of the Jews' exploration into God, his holiness was encountered first as a sense of dread in the presence of a terrifying reality. Then the Old Testament prophets made one of the great discoveries in the history of religion when they claimed to detect another element in God's holiness besides wholly otherness – moral perfection, purity, goodness, truth and justice.

The classical passage is the sixth chapter of Isaiah. That is a most majestic attempt to encapsulate the essence of holiness in words; one of the most graphic chapters not just of the Bible but in all literature. A scene of smoke and noise and blinding light; the shaking of foundations, the cry of the angels, the temple filled with unearthly presence. Isaiah reacts not just with awe and dread in the presence of God's otherness but also in despair as the human frailty of the most righteous man in the nation is exposed in the blinding presence of moral perfection like dark shadow on an X-ray screen. Against the backdrop of his contemporaries, in the half-light of human existence, Isaiah's character shone. Confronted by divine holiness, his moral being was exposed for what it was. Isaiah located his sin not as incorrect ceremonial behaviour, failure to give due honour to the Wholly Other, but in his own and his people's unclean living and evil speaking – their inability to match up to the Holy as Divine purity.

If the earliest human perceptions were of the Holy as raw energy, Isaiah encountered it as moral energy – a force which inspires good living. The Hebrew prophets summarised religion as 'the knowledge and fear of the Lord' – which believers demonstrate by a pure heart, a good conscience and sincere faith.

We have come full circle in our understanding of ultimate reality as what is supremely valuable in our lives. The holy is that which is supremely valuable for its own sake but also practically useful as an aid to living the good life. The most convincing evidence of the Holy is in the quality of our relationships, but we also acknowledge and celebrate its existence by those special rites and ceremonies which mark our togetherness.

These ceremonies, though they come to mean a great deal to us, do not take us out of the everyday world where we spend much of our lives. They do demonstrate how the Holy is mediated to us through material things. However religious we may be, we cannot fly off into the realm of the spiritual, if only because our contact with reality involves a body. We must deal with the hard and resistant stuff of things if we are to survive in the real world. It is not just our soul which needs to be kept busy in the service of the Kingdom, our senses and muscular system must also be given something to do; hence, sacraments which as material objects are fully immersed in the physical world but become charged with the values of the supernatural.

This is why great battles have been fought throughout Christian history to safeguard the doctrine of the Incarnation, which hangs on the fact that Jesus, whatever claims are made about his divine status, lived a real life, entirely human and fully contained within historical limits. He wasn't an earth-bound God-man but a Jewish carpenter who believed the earth was flat, that disease is caused by demons. He expected the world to end at any moment and put his trust in friends who let him down. And his spiritual victory depended in the last resort not on rarefied religious exercises but on the pain-inflicting power of everyday objects – wood, thorns, a spear and a handful of nails. Holy worldliness is how the life style of Jesus has been described.

Believers come to treasure sacraments and symbols as true bridges to a Holy reality. Just as the human personality needs food, space, refreshment, exercise and family affection, so does the human spirit, and it is nourished within the community of believers. The Holy both penetrates earthly things and transcends them; it is at home equally in the natural and supernatural worlds. These signs we call sacraments say to us that the power of the Holy is available to us not by way of unearthly rites but through the natural channels along which flows our energy for daily living. And because we are hyperactive creatures, they give us something to do; they demonstrate profound truths through everyday deeds – taking, breaking, eating and drinking, spilling and washing. There is nothing and yet everything mysterious about such actions.

12 SHARING THE RISK

Even in the best-run DIY clubs, members find themselves at odds. They quarrel about money and power and policy. It doesn't follow that because they have chosen to be together voluntarily in a kinship of common interest, everything is always sweetness and light. And in talking about religion as people doing things together, I've rather taken it for granted that all the dealings of the community of faith with one another are amicable. They have been doing things together in a spirit of unity and solidarity. But the harmony of mutual relationships is always likely to be broken. I do not become a member of a religious community by the spiritual equivalent of lobotomy, having a hot wire drawn across my brain to render me unfailingly cheerful and docile. My self-interest is always likely to assert itself and shatter the happy peace with its harsh demands. And this is not necessarily because I am selfish through and through. I live in a constant tension between the proper demands of my social identity and the claims of my individuality. So the religious arena will ring to the clash of wills as well as the joyous clapping of hands.

Many of the key words of theology refer to breakdowns in our common dealings and their restoration – guilt and forgiveness, estrangement and reconciliation, strife and communion, pride and penance. These great central themes of religion usually do not originate in the theological textbooks nor are they handed down directly from God by way of the preacher's rhetoric; they become real to us through the problems and pains of trying to live together.

The theologians and philosophers may puzzle over the technical terms of religion, but to most people they are merely descriptions of facts so common and universal in daily experience that they are hardly noticed. All the time, we are forgiving and being forgiven, living at odds and seeking reconciliation, knowing guilt and striving for peace of mind. A sort of skeleton scheme of theology is outlined in our daily commerce over the garden walls, across the counter and on the factory floor – to the extent that any purported relationship with God is unreal if it is not spelled out in my relationship with my neighbour; it is communing with a ghost.

If we may describe religion as something people do together, then the liability of relationships to be broken is one of its central challenges. We see this in the attitude of most religions to the fact of death. The so-called primitive religions are much taken up with rituals concerned to secure the survival of the personal spirit beyond death, and with the consequences for those left behind – the care of widows and orphans, the disposal of hereditary ranks and titles and of property. The aim is to ensure that the community can go on down the generations doing things together, even though some of its members are present only as ancestral spirits.

Breakdowns in ordinary relationships may not be as dramatic as those brought about by death but they can be very difficult to deal with. As individuals we become separated and isolated; each feels wronged by the other. When we get alienated from one another we are trapped in a vicious circle. The very state of consciousness which has produced the estrangement also makes reconciliation impossible. The power of my own self-interest is so fierce that I am prepared to reshape reality around my own ego, and the same pride which twisted things in the first place will reassert itself as I try to put things right. I will re-write history, read things that aren't there into the merest word or gesture, engage in endless self-justification, do *anything* to hold my ground and shift the blame on to the other person.

Rows and quarrels may be part of what being human means, to be expected and dealt with as best we can. But if religion is about people doing things together, because ultimate reality is to be found through their fellowship, then it takes not two but three to quarrel. God is brought into it because in shattering the fellowship we have to that extent diminished him. This is why Paul and the other writers of New Testament epistles were so stern about the squabbles in the early Christian communities. It wasn't just a matter of setting a bad example in the community or of Christians not practising what they preached, the danger was that they lost their hold on God, for as the epistle of John puts it, 'He who does not love his brother whom he has seen, cannot love God whom he has not seen' (1 John 4:20).

Religion must find a mechanism to settle breakdowns in relationship by changing our state of consciousness and restoring our fellowship with God. Such problems must have a solution because the thing is always happening. After analysing all the multiplicity of forms of religion and varieties of religious experience, William James said that underlying them all were two very simple facts: there is something wrong with us as we stand and we can only be saved from wrongness by making a proper connection with the higher power.

To put it in more traditional language, any worthwhile religion must above all offer the possibility of forgiveness. So far I've used the term God in a very broad and general way. This was inevitable because my argument has been the very basic one: that through religion, from its most primitive forms upwards, we human beings have been dealing with an unseen, supernatural, ultimate Purpose. But no religion which offered a God of philosophical generalities ever survived for long. True religion lives by precise statements about the nature and character of God, not by vague pious hopes that there is such a being.

Forgiveness introduces a new and commanding element into the definition of God. Indeed, Christianity could be defined as the belief in a God who forgives through Jesus Christ. And those whose fellowship we share confirm that we are not deluded. They insist it is possible to think of a forgiving God because, when they first base their lives on him, they become convinced they have been forgiven. This realisation changes their life, and as they change, so the world itself seems to change into a much more hopeful and astonishing place.

So one of the most important things religious people do together is to demonstrate what it means to be forgiven. In this sense, we cannot have God without our neighbours because they provide us with working models of forgiveness. In believing themselves forgiven, they have made the discovery that the only way they can narrow the gap between themselves and God is to move closer to their neighbour.

There can be no forgiveness apart from the community of forgiving and forgiven believers. This is the channel through which forgiveness reaches us; indeed, were it not for the teaching and experience of this group, we would not even know what the forgiveness of God means. People doing things together generate the psychological atmosphere where forgiveness is credible – by first-hand accounts of what has happened to them and by practising forgiveness in their dealings with one another. It is this which marks off communities of faith from other societies where members deal with one another with fairness, justice or even generosity, yet the notion that their mutual relations should have life-changing significance would never occur to them. Nor need it. They are not in the business of putting people at peace with the universe and bringing them into harmony with ultimate reality.

When I described religion as something people do together, I insisted that it was only in our togetherness that we are fully human – our humanity is located in our relationships. To remain unforgiven is to be living out a sentence of death which operates by cutting us off from those who are our link with ultimate reality. This sense of alienation is deepened by fear and produces despair, 'sickness unto death' as the philosopher Kierkegaard called it. When the community accepts us and treats us forgivingly they are offering us back our humanity. It is an invitation to rejoin the human race.

I think this is what Jesus meant when he told his disciples, 'If you forgive the sins of any, they are forgiven; if you retain the sins of any, they are retained.' This is not an endorsement of ecclesiastical authority, giving the Church power to exclude sinners from the benefits of salvation; it is a statement of fact. If I've done something wrong which cuts me off from the community of faith, and I can find no one within it who will offer me pardon and reconciliation, then my sense of alienation deepens and I lose any faith in God's forgiveness. I do not receive because I do not ask and I do not ask because I have been treated as beyond forgiveness by those from whom almost all my knowledge of God comes.

To go any further down this track must take us out of the world of religion into that of the great religions with their distinctive schemes of salvation, so I must leave the question of forgiveness at that – but not without a sense of unease at the riskiness of this whole exercise. We have been discussing a great structure of religious ideas whose crown is the possibility of a forgiving God, and it all seems to hang by a thread. We may have a strong feeling shared by many others that in talking about God we are describing something real, but there is no incontrovertible proof to back our hunch.

When the theologian Paul Tillich with his powerful mind and intricate view of reality puts the whole issue of faith in one luminous phrase, 'Just accept that you are accepted', he cuts through all the complexities with an invitation that seems too easy and too good to be true. The very simplicity of his words underlines the starkness of the option we must face.

From the outset it's been a gamble that my DIY project has any reality at all. Is what I am seeking to construct worth the time and energy I'm putting into it? Perhaps it's all a castle of cards, a monument to my patience and persistence but liable to crash down in disarray at the first breath of wind. There's an element of risk involved in most human enterprises, certainly the ones that count for anything. What degree of risk am I taking in choosing to be a religious believer, in putting my faith in a forgiving God?

The French philosopher Pascal stated the issue in just those terms, as a form of wager. We must decide what our gains and losses would be if we should stake everything on God's existence. If we win, we gain eternal life; if we lose, we lose nothing at all – since oblivion is the obvious alternative. If there is only one chance in a million of God existing, it is still better to stake everything on the remote possibility, because a finite loss is nothing compared to the chance of an infinite gain. So, asks Pascal, what have we to lose?

But Pascal's wager only makes sense if belief in God is a live option anyway. A live option is one where both possibilities are real starters. If someone were to say to me, 'Be either a Flat-Earther or a Moon Worshipper', I would shrug my shoulders, the issue is a dead one; I'm not tempted by either possibility. But if the choice is between being a Christian or an agnostic, then the option is a live one, I could conceivably be either.

Choices can also be momentous or trivial. I can choose to watch television or go out to the cinema; that's a trivial option because nothing much hangs on it, and, indeed, if the TV programmes are awful I can change my mind and go to a late showing of a film at the local cinema. But if Christopher Columbus had said to me, 'Sail with me and we'll discover a whole new world!' and I decided to stay at home and tend my garden, the option I went for would be momentous and irreversible. Jesus told a parable which made the same point. Some of those invited to the feast of the Kingdom cried off saying they'd married a wife or bought some oxen or had to look over a property and couldn't attend – choices that seemed fairly well-balanced either–ors at the time but which proved to be of the utmost significance.

It is rarely our minds which make these momentous choices between options. We don't usually believe things we have no use for. I'm unlikely to put much store in the belief that the rays given off by a crystal of magnetite can cure cancer when I'm young and bursting with health, but when the doctors pronounce my growth inoperable and send me home to die, I may decide that the crystal-ray hypothesis is at least worth putting to the test, even though the scientists say the evidence is inconclusive. My convictions can obviously be affected and changed by my feelings.

Every piece of evidence pointing to God's existence can be balanced by another casting doubt on it. The sceptic who says he hasn't got enough evidence to make up his mind is, in Pascal's terms, backing the field against the religious hypothesis. He is saying that his fear of being wrong is more important to him than his hope of being right. Certainly, he will make no mistake if he holds off committing himself until he is absolutely sure, but he will also pass up the chance of a new, exciting existence which may turn out to be eternal in quality.

Making the most modest of claims, we can say that religion is a live hypothesis which might be true. And we have the right to believe at our own risk any hypothesis that might be true. In this mortal life, no bell will toll, no heavenly light encircle our heads to signal the presence of divine truth. If we wait until we *know*, we shall already have cast our vote against religion, for just as to believe is to act in one way, to be in doubt is to act in another.

The only way of refusing to believe something is to act as though it were untrue. If I'm not sure I can trust you, I will share nothing significant about myself with you, and practically, that is tantamount to distrusting you. If I refuse to lend a hand bailing out a sinking rowing boat because I doubt it's possible to keep it afloat, I'm actively helping to sink her. Whilst I make up my mind, life has settled the issue. I may hold off making up my mind about the reality of God, but I cannot delay making up my life.

Why should it be credulous or silly to assume that if our religious needs cannot be satisfied by the world of our senses there is another world from whose reality they can be satisfied? What is improbable about such a hypothesis? Science can't pronounce againt us. She can only tell us what is, not what isn't. She can declare what she has found in the small circle of light cast by human knowledge but cannot go further and catalogue all the things that cannot possibly lie in the vast area of darkness beyond.

William James once formulated a rule about all this. He wrote, 'Always believe what is in line with your needs.'[23] It sounds like the elevation of wishful thinking to the status of a theological doctrine, but it's worth pondering. He offers the example of a man climbing a mountain who has got himself into such a position that he can only escape by a mighty leap across a crevasse. If he has faith that the leap is possible he has already added to the probability he will succeed; if he trembles and doubts and hesitates, then launches himself in a moment of despair, he has already subtracted from his chances of success because his beliefs are in opposition to his needs.

Much of life has to be lived not in terms of a firm 'Yes' or 'No' but of one 'Perhaps' after another. So far as human beings stand for anything beyond the barest biological realities, they run the risk of being mistaken; all human creativity, enterprise and discovery begins with a brave Perhaps that may end in a crashing No! But it's conceivable that our faith in the possibility of success may make the result come true. Just as the essence of courage is to stake one's life on a possibility, so the essence of faith is to believe that the possibility exists.

Of course, there are things in the universe absolutely determined once and for all regardless of what I may think, believe or fear. I cannot add one inch to my height by thinking myself taller nor can I hold back the sunrise by dreading the coming day. But there is a whole range of experience where an element of personal contribution enters into the equation. If a future fact would be quite different but for my present faith, and the result is devoutly to be desired, then it is foolish not to believe in line with my convictions provided there is no solid evidence to the contrary.

Our active preferences are an essential part of the game of life, for sometimes the only proof that something is so reveals itself after we have acted. Jesus recommended this principle as a jumping-off point for faith. The first demand he made on his followers wasn't that they should worship him or think beautiful thoughts about him but that they should follow him: 'Do what I command,' he insisted. Act like a believer. We desire greatly that God should exist, that goodness is a reality and reality is good, so we act as though it were all so and see what happens.

To act as if God exists is to pray as if there is someone who hears our prayers. It is to love our neighbour as if God himself had commanded it. It is to live in the present as if we were destined to live for ever. That is how G. K. Chesterton became a Christian. Though prayer meant nothing to him personally, he took it up as a discipline because it meant a lot to godly people whose character and spirit he admired. He hoped that by living as if prayer worked he might get the point. And he did.

Only on the day of judgement or such other denouement as the universe determines will it be revealed whether I have been vindicated or exposed as living in a fool's paradise. So be it. Even if religion proves to have been an illusion, it has given point and purpose to my life, caused me to stand as best I can for the good, the beautiful and the true and add a mite to the amount of love in the world.

13 PUTTING IT ALL TOGETHER

I must remind myself of what I decided at the beginning of this project: I've been exploring what it means to start a religion, not trying to invent a God. You can have religions without God – Buddhism, for instance, or God without religion, pantheism – the belief that the Divine is everything and everything is Divine so there's no point in having any particular area of life marked off from the rest and labelled religious. Hence there's no necessary connection between God and religion.

But neither God without religion nor religion without God makes much sense to me. It is my personal conviction and has been for a long time that there is a God whose world this is and whose nature is love. I can't prove that beyond a shadow of a doubt precisely because from time to time I have my periods of doubt. You could say that I've taken Pascal's wager, occasionally regretting it, sometimes convincing myself I have backed a loser, but on balance discovering, not so much through a set of beliefs as in an imaginative vision of things, that God is there and vindicates my trust in him.

Is there, then, a better way of expressing my trust in God than the one in which I grew up or in those which other great religions offer me? If all those old sign-posts marking the dangerous path to God were torn down, could I find my way there using navigational aids of my own devising? To use a crude DIY analogy which ought not to be pushed very far: if I lost the radio set I inherited, could I put one together which would pick up signals from the transmitter?

The theologian Don Cupitt, in a fascinating *Guardian* article, speculated on the possibility of abolishing overnight all existing religious institutions, wiping the slate clean and starting again. He fears the churches are much too committed to prolonging the religious thought of the past to create the religion of the future. He writes, 'They could only embark on the task if they were ready to allow that nothing is sacrosanct, and everything is negotiable.' And Dr Cupitt summarises the possible outcome as 'a kind of Green Christian humanism perhaps, or maybe the sort of mix of Buddhism, environmentalism and new therapies that are already familiar on the Alternative scene'.[24]

That would be a much more drastic exercise than the one I've been engaged on, for, in honesty, not everything is negotiable for me. In particular, for me, my faith in God is not negotiable. I see no point in arguing it down to a spasm of spirituality. My faith could prove not to be tough enough to stand the racketing of a hard world or might just die naturally, so that one morning I wake up and find I no longer believe. In that case, I hope I would have the courage to admit the fact and become an honest atheist. I respect and I'm a little in awe of those for whom everything in religion is negotiable, but I'm not one of them. I'm not interested in a religious DIY project which excludes the possibility of God. For me that would be Hamlet without the Prince, music without a melody, meaning without a Meaner. My radio set might make a tolerable ornament but if I were convinced that radio waves didn't exist, I'd rather get right out of the DIY radio business and construct something quite different.

If all this were just an exercise, I would by now have arrived at a crossroads. Ahead lie the paths along which the great religions invite me to travel. And all kinds of things might affect my choice: my culture and background, the place where I was brought up, the influence of my parents and friends. I might be temperamentally drawn to this great religious figure or that – Moses or Jesus or Buddha or Guru Nanak or Muhammad. I admire the humane service and self-sacrifice of the Friends, say, or the Salvation Army or the holy panache and wit of the Muslim Sufis or the Jewish

Hasidim. Arguments and theories might have their place, the books I have read, the religious music and art which inspired me, the saints who have crossed my path.

I could also stand at that crossroads and with proper caution say, 'The evidence is not all in; I'm not yet convinced that I should move from this spot until I know there is no dead-end round the next bend or ten miles ahead.' That is a position I have every right to take, so long as I remember that life drives on. Some hypotheses can be proved or disproved in five minutes; others might take longer than a life-time. God, eternity, the purpose of the universe, the meaning of life – these are big questions. By the time I *know* the truth about them beyond a reasonable shadow of a doubt, there may not be much left of my earthly span in which to enjoy my near-certainty.

But in real life it doesn't work like that. For if I stand at a crossroads at all, it is with my suitcase already packed – indeed, I'm loaded to the gunnels with baggage of one kind or another. It's that suitcase word again – *religere*; whatever holds everything together in my life. And in that bag are all my previous attempts to make sense of things, the debris of DIY projects I started and then abandoned or discarded because they wore out or I found I'd outgrown them.

Indeed, I've changed the size of my luggage several times in my life-time. In my traditional phase, it would have taken a cabin trunk to carry the wealth of theological ideas, doctrines and dogmas I ascribed to. With the blush of a theological college education fresh upon my cheeks, name a doctrine the Church Fathers smiled upon and I believed it, especially if it had a long name. Then in the Swinging Sixties, a slender brief-case or even a capacious wallet would have held the skeletal creed I thought was enough to get me through in the era of religionless Christianity. Now it's a medium-sized suitcase again, but its contents are much more varied.

For customs purposes I would have to declare that my suitcase contained not just orthodox Christian convictions but some truths about the African world-view derived from my years in Zambia. Some of its contents, too, would be strictly kosher. As a follower of Jesus of Nazareth I always had a proper respect for Judaism, out my research for a book about religious humour took me to the writings of those Jewish sages and saints, the Hasidim. I ended up with an awareness of Jesus's Jewishness so intense I could almost taste it. My consciousness of Christianity's origin as an oriental apocalyptic movement has permeated all my religious thinking since. And in a time of theological laissez-faire, the Muslims' fierce defence of God's honour has been a hot desert blast on my rather wet theism.

So, I've made a number of fresh starts in shaping my faith, though always using the same Christian template as a basis. You might say I'm playing with words, I haven't started again, merely modified or developed my theological views to keep up with my experience of life. To an outsider, that's how it might seem, just a reshuffling of my religious ideas; to me, each change was a revel-ation, a new experience of God which entailed a reappraisal of all else in my religion. The people of Israel learned the hard way that when they tried to hoard manna it went sour. We can hang on to religious truth only by constantly reacquiring it. Faith only exists as a continuous inner warfare; like love and freedom, we have to win it over and over again.

It's like one of those posers antique dealers have to wrestle with – how many parts of an original piece of furniture can be replaced before it ought no longer to be called a Sheraton? Sir Herbert Butterfield in the final sentence of his Reith lectures, *Christianity and History*, coined a memorable dictum, 'Hold to Christ, and for the rest be totally uncommitted.'[25] I'm not sure that takes account of the blessed suitcase. The invitation to dump our accumulated baggage is a beguiling one. But it's not just any old rummage in there, some of the things are vital to my identity. Every refugee I encountered in Africa carried at least one pathetic little bundle which marked out his or her individuality from the rest of the endless tide of anonymous humanity.

Many of us start a new religion at least once in our lives because we are unique, unrepeatable human beings and therefore when we do something for the first time, it has never been done before. No one else in the entire history of the universe has walked in our footsteps or occupied exactly the same space, time and condition we enjoy or endure. That precise combination of ignorance and knowledge, trust and doubt, hope and despair is ours alone. As the old rabbi said, 'God never does the same thing twice.' Every act of creation, including the one that brings each one of us into being, is an original. As I've made clear, in the religious trade, unlike many other areas of busines, we cannot act through agents; we cannot pay people to discover God on our behalf – not even if they wear clerical collars or occupy university chairs of theology. Everybody must make his or her own estimate of the meaning and point of life, and then turn it into a truth to live by. And that exploration into God, that journey and experience, is our peculiar path, however much the sheep-dogs of official religion snap at our heels and try to drive us along pre-determined routes.

If I have no general view of existence, if I'm sleep-walking through religion, I'm like someone who spends months drawing a detailed ordinance map of the country between London and Manchester and never discovers that Britain is an island. I wake up when something makes me take my nose off the paper, pull back and see the total outline of Britain. I realise that Britain is an island not by a detailed examination of the terrain, but in a flash of perception: everything in its proper place and to the correct perspective.

Our personal religion starts when we come awake to the power over us of what we supremely value, what we have set our hearts upon above all else. 'Awakening' is a common gospel expression for being brought up against the presence of grace. We start our own religion the first time we realise we have one; when we stop sleep-walking through the religion bequeathed to us by our parents or convention and affirm, 'Yes, that I do (or do not) believe!'

The experience of coming awake doesn't at all resemble those painstaking DIY projects where we put things together systematically in the correct order. It's unusual for us to get the point by going through a check-list, like a pilot in the cockpit of an aeroplane ensuring that everything is in working order for take-off. We don't judiciously decide how our religion rates as a system of explanation that gives a coherent account of life and our own place in it whether its ethics are up to scratch and enable us to live by those moral qualities we have found anchor us in reality. We may do a consumer-test on a religion to see whether there is friendship and warmth as well as discipline and purpose; to judge how good the singing, praying and preaching are. But that is rarely decisive.

Take Christianity as the example best known to me. Christians usually come awake religiously when their attitude to Jesus changes. That's how everything else in Christianity falls into place, not normally in an instant, in a cut and dried mental decision, though that can happen, but as a result of many perceptions of him from a lot of different angles, an accumulation of ideas and opinions about him and often the personal experiences of others who have undergone this change in attitude.

When the people of Jesus's time met him, a blessed few seemed to be encountering transcendent love, moral judgement, grace and forgiveness, calling and command. They realised they were as near as they were going to get to God, to seeing the Infinitely Invisible and hearing the Eternally Silent speak. And enough people of our time feel the same about him to inspire others to take a much closer look at him.

If we do take a closer look at Jesus, we soon realise that any faith based upon him is like one of those DIY projects where the regularity of design is disturbed because real life has twists and turns that don't conform to the theoretical pattern. C. S. Lewis puts it like this: 'Reality is usually something you could not have guessed. That is one of the reasons why I believe Christianity. If it offered us just the kind of universe we had always expected, I should feel we were making it up. It has just that queer twist about it that real things have.'[26]

There are secret irregularities in real life which every DIY enthusiast ignores at his peril. There is also a strange but decisive twist in Christian truth which if we were inventing our own religion we would never have thought to put in our plan. No doubt, other great religions also have these critical deviations from the standard patterns of reality, but I can speak only for the faith I know best.

The unexpected twist in the Christian story becomes apparent the moment we give Jesus a close look. It is the cross. Not because violent death or martyrdom were unusual or unexpected fates to befall a religious prophet. Given the uncompromising things Jesus said and did, it would have been against the odds had he died in his bed. That is not the problem. It is the way the whole of Christianity is poised like a great pyramid on this point. It's clear that what founded Christianity was not the teaching or even the life of Jesus but the preaching of his death and resurrection. The last week of Jesus's life and his death takes up more of the gospel story than the other twenty odd years of his life put together. In fact, it is the dominant theme of the entire New Testament. The illogicality seems to be that the one they called the Lord of Life came to die.

Christianity's basic building regulation has only one master-clause: God was in Christ reconciling the world to himself. That's what holds the whole structure together. The claim is that in Jesus the ultimate sustaining framework of reality which encompasses everything became visible and by an act of self-sacrifice he showed that its nature is love. It is asserted that this disclosure was not confined to a single brief historical episode. The God who was revealed in him reproduces the likeness of Jesus in successive generations of Christians.

That is a proposition one can quite reasonably reject out of hand as totally incredible, but what cannot be denied is that Christianity would be in tatters without it. The cross is the effectual sign under which Christian people meet to do things together; it provides much of the power of Christian preaching, it is the motivation for the mutual commitment of God and humanity celebrated in its sacraments.

But there is a paradox here. Though the cross of Jesus is undoubtedly the most evocative symbol of Christianity and generates much of its spiritual energy, the historical Jesus would not allow himself to be put at the centre of the picture; he pointed away from himself towards God who alone was good, for whose kingly rule he lived and died. His master-idea was the Lordship of God. It is through Jesus that Christians are put in touch with the God who is the goal of all religion, and it is a form of truncated DIY to stop short even at Jesus and say, 'Thus far and no further.' One cannot imagine the Jesus we know from the gospels allowing that. As he insisted, 'He who believes in me does not believe in me but in him who sent me.' What could be clearer or more decisive than that?

Thus when, as Christians claim, people are converted by and to Jesus, what Jesus is converting them to is God. That might seem a blinding statement of the obvious, but at a time when there is more than a whiff of Christian triumphalism in the air, it needs spelling out. And one practical result of this ought to be that we recognise as honest believers those whose path to God has cut through different cultural, geographical or historical terrain. They are not, as some theologians claim when they are trying to be kind and succeed only in being patronising, 'hidden' or 'anonymous' Christians. Many of them are theists, just as Jesus himself was. They may not share our faith in Jesus, but they share Jesus's faith in God. No one could accuse the apostle Paul of selling short the true significance of Christ, yet he very firmly tells the Christians at Corinth that in the end even Jesus will be subjected to the Father in order that God 'may be everything to everyone'. A God who is everything to everyone – that is the ultimate goal of humanity's religious search.

NOTES

1 W.R Inge. Quoted in the *International Thesaurus of Quotations*, London, Penguin, 1973
2 Wilfred Cantwell Smith in *The Myth of Christian Uniqueness*, eds. P. Knitter & J. Hicks, p. 55, London, SCM Press, 1988
3 I owe the image to John MacMurray
4 G. K. Chesterton, *Heretics*, p. 15, London, Bodley Head, 1910
5 Quoted by W. MacNeile Dixon, *The Human Situation*, p. 258, London, Edward Arnold, 1937
6 Dietrich Bonhoeffer, *Letters and Papers from Prison*, p. 21, London, SCM Press, 1971
7 C. S. Lewis, Appendix to *The Abolition of Man*, Oxford, Oxford University Press, 1943
8 Nicholas Lashin, *Is Christianity Credible?*, ed. P. Stacey, p. 21, London, Epworth Press, 1981
9 Austin Farrer, *Lord, I Believe*, p. 14, Faith Press, 1958
10 Dorothy L. Sayers, *The Mind of the Maker*, p. 76, Methuen, 1941
11 Bertrand Russell in a newspaper interview whose source I've lost
12 G. K. Chesterton, *G. K.'s Weekly*, May 1930
13 Quoted by W. P. Patterson, *The Nature of Religion*, p.200, London, Hodder & Stoughton, 1925
14 I owe some of these ideas to John MacMurray, *Freedom in the Modern World*, New Jersey, Humanities Press, 1991
15 Dorothy L. Sayers, op. cit.
16 G. K. Chesterton, *G. K.'s Weekly*, March 1929
17 W. Cantwell Smith in *Wilfred Cantwell Smith: A theology for the world*, ed. E. Hughes, p. 15, London, SCM Press, 1986
18 E. Underhill, *Man and the Supernatural*, p. 27, London, Methuen, 1927
19 A. E. Whitham, *The Pasture of his Presence*, p. 36, London, Hodder & Stoughton, 1939
20 Again John MacMurray supplied the key idea
21 Quoted in *The Mind of Chesterton*, C. Hollis, p. 69, Hollis & Carter, 1970
22 D. Z. Phillips, *The Concept of Prayer*, p. 130, London, Routledge, Kegan & Paul, 1965

23 William James, *The Will to Believe*, p. 11, Boston, Harvard University Press, 1979

24 *Guardian*, 29 February 1992

25 Herbert Butterfield, *Christianity and History*, p. 146, London, Bell, 1950

26 C. S. Lewis. I regret I failed to note the source

INDEX